Something New

Something New

Wedding Etiquette for Rule Breakers,

Traditionalists, and Everyone in Between

Elise Mac Adam

SIMON SPOTLIGHT ENTERTAINMENT

New York London Toronto Sydney

While the "Etiquette in Action" letters were inspired by questions submitted to the IndieEtiquette column at Indiebride, most are amalgams of many similar queries. In all cases, the original questions have been entirely rewritten, clarified, and made more generally applicable. Any and all potentially identifying details have been altered or excised.

S|S|E

SIMON SPOTLIGHT ENTERTAINMENT

An imprint of Simon & Schuster

1230 Avenue of the Americas, New York, New York 10020

Copyright © 2008 by Elise Mac Adam

SIMON SPOTLIGHT ENTERTAINMENT and related logo are trademarks of Simon & Schuster, Inc.

Manufactured in the United States of America

First Edition 10 9 8 7 6 5 4 3 2 1

Library of Congress Cataloging-in-Publication Data

Mac Adam, Elise.

Something new : wedding etiquette for rule breakers, traditionalists,

and everyone in between / Elise Mac Adam.

p. cm.

ISBN-13: 978-1-4169-4910-7 (alk. paper)

ISBN-10: 1-4169-4910-0 (alk. paper)

1. Wedding etiquette. I. Title.

BJ2051.M32 2008

395.2'2—dc22

2007034211

For my sturdy battalion: Stephen, Felix, Sebastian, and Mr. Sheridan

Acknowledgments

One of the pleasures of finishing this book is being able to let the people who so graciously helped see it through know how grateful I am.

Beginning at the beginning, I must thank Lori Leibovich, who took a chance on letting me invent an etiquette column for Indiebride. The whole concept of combining etiquette with the "independent" aesthetic seemed likely to draw fire as reactionary, or at least oxymoronic. Instead it has thrived. The column would not exist without its readers and letter writers, so everyone who has been following it, reading it, and writing in with their questions, complaints, and puzzlements also deserves enormous thanks.

Equally deserving of tremendous thanks is Lauren Galit, my amazing and dedicated agent—a woman who always knows what to say, who has limitless energy, interests, and patience, and who I also feel privileged to call my friend.

Christa Bourg was the first person to take my book as seriously as I did, and she not only taught me how to write a proposal for it, she also had enough faith to give it, and me, several crucial shoves. She has been a wonderful teacher and friend.

I am also deeply grateful for the interest and enthusiasm of Emily Westlake, Tricia Boczkowski, and the rest of the team at Simon Spotlight Entertainment.

For maintenance of another sort, I need to thank the people who have helped me clear all sorts of paths so I could work and live with something approaching balance: Dr. Lynn, Dr. A., Namgyal Tendol, Sarah Lavin, Maya Burzynski, and Renata Joy. For reasons both practical (of the two-legged shouting variety) and emotional, I could not have written without their assistance, cheer, and encouragement.

It is hard to write a book under a cloak of secrecy, so thanks are due to a host of friends who provided inspiration, suggestions, moral support, and the cattle prod: Jean-Christophe Castelli, Anne Watkins, Dale Hrabi, Lynn Snowden-Picket, Erroll McDonald, Maria DiBattista, Cheryl Mendelson, Ginger Strand, and mediabistro's classes of nonfiction writers.

Through all of this and much, much more I am so grateful to Gabrielle Nohrnberg, who has been an unshakable friend for so many years that delicacy prohibits precise enumeration. She has read, supported, commented, observed, and helped me along with my work, with my life, with everything.

I am sorry that one friend is not able to see my book. Siobhán Kilfeather gave me new ways to look at the world and a faith that I could wander down as many avenues as I like. I love her and hope that this book fulfills any happy thoughts she had about it.

This is a book about weddings, and in my case it would be impossible to have a wedding without family. The entire Kramarsky collective has been the greatest extended family I could have lucked into, and it is an honor to be included in their lives. (Special credit goes to Sarah-Ann Kramarsky and to Laura Kramarsky, who patiently endured my electronic rants.)

The allure of comportment blossomed for me when my father gave me an etiquette book as a divertissement to stave off middle-school ennui. I do not know if I would have been led down this path without his present, but I can promise that I owe everything to my parents, Barbara and Alfred Mac Adam, whose love has always been constant and who would do anything to encourage any amusement, project, or passion I embrace; my brother, Geoffrey Mac Adam, who has always been loving and loyal, the very best sort of sibling; and my sister-in-law, Reena Jana, a wonderful and interested friend. I love them and hope this book demonstrates the tip of the iceberg of their influence on me.

I meant it when I said that weddings are about family, and I am so grateful for my inner circle. Stephen, my husband, gave me the love, time, room, and encouragement that let me write. I love him in ways the rules of civility can't touch. Felix gave me the kick that got me started. Sebastian forced me to finish it, and Mr. Sheridan almost always had spot-on timing for comfort and distraction. Almost. I love all of my families, and the creation of this one is the best aftermath I can imagine of any wedding.

Contents

Introduction

Etiquette Is for Everyone

I didn't find the prospect of getting married daunting—at first. What did I know? I hadn't been to many weddings. My sole experience as a member of a wedding party was as a six-year-old flower girl who managed to wiggle a loose tooth out during the ceremony, but I suspected the basics were easy enough. As a guest I knew to: RSVP on time, send a present, only bring a date if one was invited, keep mum about alcohol-inspired ramblings of friends (at one wedding the only person I knew decided to tell me about her sexual liaison with the groom in the not-distant-enough past). . . . As a bride I figured everything would turn out all right if I picked a day, place, time, and dress, invited all the expected friends and relatives, and didn't get drunk and say something stupid. It all seemed very easy to someone who had never really been educated in the ways of nuptials.

Pretty thoughts, but I was oblivious. It took perhaps three telephone calls before I was overwhelmed. Planning quandaries weren't what got to me, it was the withering cloud of doubt: about the guest list, about everyone's feelings, about my idea of dolling up in pink, about the invitation language, about . . . everything. My intentions were good, but the opportunities for being unintentionally obnoxious were legion. Oddly, at the very moment when most people would be inclined to beg for help, I retreated, afraid to admit to my family, future in-laws, even friends, how awkward and uncomfortable I felt. Admitting my ignorance was embarrassing—too embarrassing to talk about. I craved some sort of guide, a handbook for making it through the wedding enterprise without becoming an alienating harridan.

I've been fascinated by manners and the rules of comportment, most of which were intriguing curiosities to me, since I was a teenager, when my father gave me an etiquette book as—I hoped—a joke. Over the years, and not with any conscious goal in mind, I had compiled a library of etiquette books, antique and contemporary. Suddenly these volumes that had previously served my private curiosity obtained a new purpose. Their protocols and policies became my life preservers.

Not coincidentally, shortly after I married, I began dedicating a large part of my life to etiquette, when I became a columnist for Indiebride, a wedding website for people who never really understood what the standard white dress, diamonds, and tulle were supposed to say to them. Years have gone by and I have responded to brides and grooms; people ending engagements; parents trying to figure out their boundaries; bridesmaids and groomsmen; colleagues, relatives, and friends; all of whom are overwhelmed by nuptial obligations and potential pitfalls.

Through the years I've developed an even deeper appreciation for etiquette, which, at its core, is a set of social guidelines and expectations. It goes much deeper than pointing out what a fish knife looks like or cautioning against wearing white shoes after Labor Day. Etiquette offers a compass when you don't know how to behave around strangers in strange lands—even if that foreign country is a house a few doors down. Embracing etiquette isn't a reactionary exercise (unless the etiquette one tries to embrace is from the seventeenth-century court of the Sun King, Louis XIV); it's practical and convenient. Most people are willing to consult maps when they don't know how to get somewhere. Consider etiquette an interpersonal map, and if any event demands such an item, it is a wedding.

Nuptial waters are rough. Brides, grooms, parents, guests, flower girls (and boys), pets—no one escapes the weird parallel universe a wedding creates, in which it is impossible to feel "normal." This makes sense because, if you think about it, weddings aren't normal. They are bigger than life—totally separate from the quotidian. How could it be otherwise? Two families are merging, which produces all kinds of competition and anxiety. Friends are reconfiguring their priorities, which also produces competition and anxiety. More than anything else, weddings demonstrate seismic change. Women become wives. Men turn into husbands. Children definitely grow up (unless they don't, in which case you can see their parents' plaintive letters in syndicated advice columns) and create their own homes and families. Weddings are endings as well as beginnings.

Family members are far from the only ones suffering from nuptial discomfort and malaise. Weddings dredge up social minefields that people don't wander into very often now that informality is celebrated and social rigidity is considered elitist and snotty. Etiquette gets its bad rap because people unfamiliar with its magic imagine it is the invention of fancy types to make the hoi polloi feel uncultured. If this is what you think, you're either sorely mistaken or have been the victim of too many coarse correctives by people who should know better. Really, etiquette provides a set of tools that everyone can use to figure out how to handle any social situation. It is not about limiting free will or anything like that. Etiquette exists to prevent hurt feelings, help you get through difficult encounters with dignity, and create order where there is otherwise a void of indecision. What do you do when you're faced with a black-tie affair and you're generally a flip-flops and jeans type? How do you reject the endless pressure to assign bridesmaids when you can't stand the idea of them? Is there a way to figure out why your hosts appear to have forgotten to invite your wife? Can you nip the outrageous competition between mother and future mother-in-law in the bud—or at least get them to stop comparing outfits?

The key to breaking etiquette out of its Victorian stereotype is to understand the two things it does *not* do. In the first place, etiquette is not about practicality. This is fine; weddings are not about practicality either. (If you want an efficient wedding, tell no one and go down to city hall.) It isn't gracious, for instance, to write on your invitations that you just want cash presents—even if you really do have at least one of everything you need for every domestic occasion and want to pay off your student loans. So, even though it might feel less squirmy and more "honest" to just print cash requests on the invitations, it comes off as greedy—and etiquette frowns on being crass.

In the second place, etiquette is not interested in making people feel small or stupid for not knowing the rules. It is designed to create *comfort*, with a standard set of protocols and expectations accessible to everyone. Scolding people unfamiliar with the intricacies of manners is rude in and of itself.

I wrote this book in the spirit of transparency. No matter how much of an iconoclast you are, if you're social enough to have a wedding, or if you were invited to a wedding, or were asked to be in a wedding party, or if you happen to be related to the prospective bride or groom—you're going to run into questions of etiquette. There is no escape, so you might as well embrace the life preserver. What you need to know is how to make the rules of etiquette work to your advantage while ditching the ones that don't apply to you, and this is tricky when the advice hurtling your way from friends and magazines and books and the Internet is contradictory, inflexible, and occasionally hard to understand.

Modern weddings are full of nontraditional families, strange circumstances, and odd and offbeat issues. How do you fit the names of all parents and step-parents onto your invitation? How do you address an invitation to a couple where the husband took his wife's last name? Can you refuse to be in the wedding party if you're afraid of dogs and the best man is a Rhodesian ridgeback? The mystery is the scary part. The relief is that all questions have answers. The one thing everyone involved in any kind of wedding deserves is clarity and, yes, under all the pomp and ceremony and tears and tulle, you can find comfort and security in a set of general guidelines for politeness.

Form and Function:
How This Book Works

If the word "etiquette" still smacks too strongly of elitism and rigidity, prepare to overcome your prejudices.

Treat this book as a primer and glean information while following the standard wedding chronology, starting with the engagement—the moment a wedding becomes a twinkle in someone's eye—all the way through to the end (whether that means thank-you note writing or some worst-case scenario troubleshooting). Each chapter advises not only the wedding couple, but also anyone who has been stung by the nuptial bug: guests, members of the wedding party, relatives, people who weren't even invited but who would like to have been—everyone can find wedding recourse inside these pages.

Each chapter begins with a discussion and list of *Traditional Basics*. These are the standard policies and practices that have been exercised for many decades. In addition to the obvious advantage of being vaguely familiar with them so that you'll know what other people are talking about when they inquire about certain ancient traditions, you'll get a sense as to why they exist in the first place. That way you can see why some may work well for you while others might not apply to your life or circumstances, and then you can prepare civilized arguments against the points that don't suit your situation.

Many traditions need to be adapted to take the vicissitudes of contemporary life into account. To that end, *Traditional Basics* are followed by a longer section called *Twisting Tradition,* which includes discussions of pitfalls that the etiquette doyennes of previous centuries could have only dreamed of having to negotiate, and offers polite, modern variations on old rules.

Finally, each chapter ends with *Etiquette in Action*, demonstrations of how etiquette can be applied to complicated situations. This section contains letters and responses inspired by real questions I have been asked. Sometimes it can be easier to see how to make etiquette work for you if you see how it has worked for others, instead of trying to imagine your predicament fitting under the standard umbrella of rules.

What Etiquette Can and Can't Do

Etiquette will rescue you from social disaster. It will ease stressful circumstances. But it can't make everyone happy all the time. Inevitably you will make choices that will annoy people. Maybe you will opt for a child-free wedding, which will offend the parents of the excluded tots on your guest list. Perhaps you will decide that medical school won't give you the time off to be a bridesmaid, which will hurt the bride's feelings. You might want to invite your entire bridge club, which will enrage your son, the groom. If you don't want to go to a destination wedding, your hosts could wonder why you stopped liking them. This can't be helped. People, whether they are members of the wedding or innocent bystanders, should only have to sacrifice so much free will.

Learn what your choices are in various nuptial situations, how to calculate how much each option is worth, and whether the price is financial or emotional. You will have all sorts of contradictory influences, and you have to figure out not only what you want, but whether you want to have it your way at all costs. There are polite ways, for instance, to tell people you're having a child-free wedding, but only you can decide whether the repercussions of prohibiting the underage set are worth it to you. And perhaps there's a different battle you'd rather win. In short, there are ways to finesse all sorts of situations, but it is up to you to know when you want to play your cards, and what's the best and most polite way to play them. You won't be able to win all the time.

Etiquette works. It thrives in spite of the miserable taunts it must endure and the injustice of its bad reputation. Everyone needs it. You need it. So whether you are a maverick or play things strictly by the book, there are manners old and new that will see you though, for better or worse.

Chapter 1

Plunging In: Getting Engaged and Opening Pandora's Box

Marriage proposals have gotten so overhyped, it is a miracle anyone gets it together to pop the question anymore. There's so much pressure to be original and creative, yet spontaneous and romantic, that the performance alone is almost more daunting than the threat of a "No." On the other side of the velvet box, proposal recipients often hope the question will arrive like a bolt from the blue in the form of a dazzling, exciting, glamorous surprise. The irony for both parties is that rarely does a marriage proposal come as a total shock, and there are some who would question the wisdom of completely unforeseen proposals in the first place.

Happily, there is no standard protocol for asking someone to marry you. The territory is wide open, although there are some favorite clichés: kneeling by candlelight, a proposal proffered in Parisian twilight, a sparkling ring served on top of a chocolate soufflé. The walls of tradition don't really start closing in until after the tearfully ecstatic "Yes" has been uttered. From then on you're caught in the nuptial maze that you'll have to navigate, at least until the last thank-you note is written.

But the fun hasn't even started yet.

Traditional Basics

Asking

- Someone asks and someone else says yes. Traditionally, the prospective groom does the asking, and the answering falls to the future bride.

- If he is feeling extremely traditional, the future groom approaches the prospective bride's family, specifically her father, to ask for his permission before he even broaches the subject with the woman he loves. This can happen in person or over the telephone. If he has already proposed, the future groom can still approach the bride's family members for their blessing. If they refuse to sanction the union, the future bride has to decide whether or not to go ahead and get married anyway and hope that her family will eventually come around.

- The groom presents the bride with an engagement ring. This often happens as part of the proposal. He can also offer an inexpensive "place holder" ring so that the bride can take part in ring selection. (Baubles made with cubic zirconia are popular for this purpose.) Engagement rings do not have to feature large diamonds. (Diamonds have only been "traditional" since the DeBeers empire started the trend in the mid-twentieth century, anyway.) They also don't have to be outrageously expensive. The whole notion that an engagement ring should cost the equivalent of "two months' salary" is a tradition ripped off from an advertising campaign, which should tell you something about how much you want to participate in it.

After the Acceptance

- Once it has been determined that the bride is willing to take the plunge, the bride and groom notify their families of the happy news. It is assumed that the parents or guardians of the Couple in Question are at least aware that their children are involved with each other. This ostensibly makes everything else a happy surprise, not a shock.

- Standard procedure is for the groom's parents to introduce themselves to the bride's family, but if the bride's parents get tired of waiting, they can make the first move without being considered presumptuous or feeling annoyed that the groom's family was sluggish. These are early days and everyone should be pleased that things are trundling along and not look for reasons to get feathers in a ruffle.

- As for a time frame, there are no rules about how long engagements should or should not be. Keep in mind, however, that the longer the engagement, the longer you will have to field questions about the wedding.

Announcing

- The wedding couple should tell family and close friends and anyone who would be hurt not to hear the happy news from the horses' mouths. Wider circles can learn about the engagement through what the tome *Social Etiquette of New York,* written in the late nineteenth century, calls "good-natured gossip."

- Engagement announcements can be made at celebratory dinners or parties. These events are not necessary, but they get the word out quickly.

- Many newspapers publish engagement announcements, which can be used to broadcast the news on a large scale.

- The couple should not mail out printed cards announcing the engagement. This tends to look odd, as if they are sending out a signal to start sending them presents.

- The engagement should not be announced if either the future bride or the future groom is still married to someone else, in any sense, at all.

Twisting Tradition

Now that the landscape of tradition has been set before you, your mind is surely reeling. Your experience doesn't fit the classical structure. Your family doesn't conform to anything remotely "normal," and the strangeness of your engagement is suddenly frightening where it once felt carefree. Etiquette is supposed to be useful, and there are always ways to let tradition inspire you, no matter how staunchly progressive you are.

Anyone Can Ask

Would you rather ask the question or be in charge of the answer? Does neither situation appeal to you? Tradition has men making the proposal while women are charged with "green-lighting" it (or not), but there's no reason this has to be the case. Proposal roles don't have to break down along gender lines. This logic obviously holds for same-sex couples. In fact, it is more reasonable if each job goes to the person who is most suited to it, temperamentally speaking.

If neither party is interested in taking the lead, couples can mutually decide to get married. Rarely is a proposal a total shocker, and the only possible pitfall you could face is that in the months preceding the wedding you might not have a snappy anecdote to recount when people ask about your "proposal story." (Proposal stories are a bit overrated anyway. The best ones should be largely indescribable in polite company either because of their salaciously romantic details or because they are full of in-jokes only the wedding couple could appreciate.) Do what feels comfortable, not what you think the world expects you to do. You aren't marrying the world; you're just living in it.

Engagement Rings and . . . Things

In many circles, the moment a woman says she's engaged, hands grab at her, eager to fondle and admire the ring that proves it. What's wrong with this picture? Only *everything*. In the first place, one doesn't need an engagement ring for an engagement to be legit. Of course you can propose without a ring. The only thing you need is someone to propose *to*.

If you decide to get an engagement ring, keep in mind that you have nothing to prove. There are no real traditions that you can violate, and anyone who suggests otherwise has been brainwashed by a couple of powerful advertising campaigns that are less than a hundred years old. Engagement rings can feature any number of stones that are or are not diamonds (or they can be completely rock free). Size does not matter. If you like your ring and compatriots see fit to sneer at it, remember three things: (1) You're the one wearing it; (2) You aren't the one who looks covetous, greedy, or obnoxious; and (3) At this stage it's easy to strike any and all snarkers off the guest list.

What's that? You say you have an allergy to all precious metal? No one *needs* a ring, but exchanging engagement presents has an obvious appeal. There's no need to ditch the gesture just because jewelry doesn't do it for you. So, what sounds good to you? Do you each want to get a watch because you're both chronically late? Do you have a joint fascination you can feed with deluxe camping equipment or cookware, additions to your library, hang-gliding apparatus, or something else that speaks to you about your relationship? Anything goes, and it should go without saying that it is nice when both halves of the wedding couple can receive an engagement bonus.

What Do You Mean, Ask **Permission?**

What's that sound? It is the collective gasp of independent people who cringe at the idea that a decision as personal as getting married must be sanctioned by the parents. The entire notion seems backward and antiquated, like a throwback to times when women waited under their fathers' roofs for men to come and establish them in a different sort of circumstance.

As long as you're of age and meet the other requirements of your jurisdiction, you don't need anyone's permission to get married. There is, however, something sweet about the tradition of including the parents that might still retain a flicker of interest.

Autonomy is one of the great pleasures of being an adult, and this independence gives you the power to be gracious. You certainly don't have to get permission from anyone, but it never hurts to throw the parents a bone, particularly if you are secure in the knowledge that they can't do anything to stop you. This is particularly the case if you are dealing with parents who feel strongly attached to tradition.

So instead of going to a father and asking for his daughter's hand in marriage, you can level the playing field. If you and your partner have decided to get married but want to preserve something of the courtly courtesy that asking permission offers, consider approaching both sets of parents and speaking to them soberly about your plans and let them know how much you hope they share your happiness. Speaking to them this way will create the impression that you are hoping they'll approve while simultaneously letting them know that you've already made your decision. You haven't had to compromise; all the parents feel respected; everyone's happy.

Meeting of the Minds: The Parents

Tradition places family introductions squarely in the laps of the parents, but parents, being human, can be busy, shy, intimidated, or antisocial. In the face of those obstacles, why leave it up to the people who are most likely to be ham-fisted and embarrassing? Anyone can take charge of this crucial moment and stage the meeting him- or herself.

All sorts of issues can threaten to create stumbling blocks between remaining separate families and becoming a joined (even if by force) unit: distance, time, cultural traditions, personality quirks . . . but none of these should matter. If you can't get everyone together early in your engagement for a big formal get-together, snag some time right before your wedding for a casual meeting. You can have a parents' lunch, dinner, tea, or cocktails at your place. The idea is not to create "one big happy family" but to do something very practical: make your families a little more comfortable with each other. They don't have to be best friends, but ideally they won't be total strangers at the wedding.

Announcing

For the most part, the traditional policies on engagement announcements make sound, practical sense. They allow the information to spread naturally, through word-of-mouth or social osmosis (as in: Your old friend from your eighth-grade soccer team will write to you full of congratulations because her mother clipped your engagement notice out of the local paper and sent it to her in Australia, where she's living the good life).

═══════ *Etiquette in Action* ═══════

CAN'T MAKE ME TELL

Dear Elise,

My boyfriend proposed. I accepted. My future mother-in-law (with whom I don't get along) asked to hear the proposal story. I told her that it was a private moment. Her feelings were hurt, but it's none of her business. I think it is good to set boundaries. Was I wrong?

—Private Person

Dear Private,

People are always asked how they got engaged. Why else would people commission "Marry Me" ads in newspapers and at sporting events, or serve up diamond rings drowning in flutes of champagne? Getting engaged can involve a very public display of very private feelings. This makes sense when one keeps in mind that marriage in itself involves signing a contract that becomes a public record. It is announcing to the world that you are committed to each other.

Your fiancé's mother was asking how he proposed, not begging for a description of the circumstance under which you conceived her grandchild. Her question was neither weird nor nosey, and for you to treat it this way actually *was* rather rude, or at the very least off-putting.

I'm not telling you to cave to her whims, but even if your future mother-in-law was being wildly intrusive, there are ways to handle her question gently:

o Be demure: "He was very sweet, and all I could do was say yes."
o Take a "just the facts, ma'am" approach: "Well, we went out for a fabulous dinner at this bistro we love, and he asked me to marry him. You know, they make their frites with a little bit of cayenne pepper and they are so incredibly delicious. Have you tried them?"
o Be coy: "Well, it was really a surprise, and now I'm just so excited. Was this a surprise to you, too?"

You were uncharitably aggressive. Perhaps she was just trying to seem interested in your happy moment. Maybe she was taking your engagement as an opportunity to try to mend some fences with you. What did you hope to accomplish in being so harsh? This woman is your fiancé's *mother*, and even if you don't want to open your heart to her, you could have been kind without revealing what you feel are tender emotions that aren't her business.

If you want to smooth her feathers, it wouldn't take much to apologize for being short and give her a tidbit of general information that you don't mind her knowing.

THEY WON'T TRAVEL

Dear Elise,

My fiancé and I want our families to meet before the wedding, and my family wants to meet his, but his family is really resistant.

In my mother's culture, tradition dictates that the groom's family must visit the bride's family. If they don't, my mother will believe that they have no respect for me. We invited his family to visit and offered to pay for everything, but they say that they can't take time off work. My fiancé suspects they will be reluctant to attend our wedding. How do I approach them and emphasize how important their visit is?

—Resenting the In-Laws

Dear Resenting,

This issue is not simply about cultural differences, but there is only so much you can do, short of drugging your fiancé's parents and forcing them on a plane.

Has your fiancé discussed with his parents how important their visit is? Has he asked them why they don't want to travel? They should hear in simple terms how important this gesture would be to their son, to you, and to your mother.

Maybe they do understand and they simply don't want to travel. This is their prerogative, but they could soften their choice somewhat by writing to your mother. Your fiancé could urge them to do this, or perhaps they could send a token present. In turn, you should work on your mother to convince her that your fiancé's parents mean no insult.

Finally, you should take charge and create your own meeting. Arrange a lunch or dinner for just you, your fiancé, and both sets of parents before the wedding. If this means that your fiancé's parents need to show up a day early for the wedding, so be it. If they absolutely won't travel even for your wedding, I'm afraid I'm out of suggestions. They may be phobic in some way they can't admit, or there may be other, darker reasons for their reluctance to budge. These are things you can't control, so if you've tried everything, you must keep in mind that it isn't your job to make everyone happy, and regardless of what happens, you should enjoy your own happy engagement and marriage.

Chapter 2

The Root of All Evil: Money

Nothing sends heady postengagement nuptial fantasies crashing to earth faster than a quick budgetary assessment. It doesn't matter whether you've embraced the Wedding-Industrial Complex and have a three-foot-high stack of wedding magazines doubling as your night table, or have barely given your wedding a second thought since you got engaged. Unless you're getting married at city hall with no frills or are in the happy position of never needing to look at a price tag, you will need to compromise and negotiate.

In point of fact, even if one is not a bride or groom but is "merely" a parent, a bridesmaid, a friend, a groomsman, or a flower boy's mother, one will need to sharpen those bargaining skills . . . and take at least a cursory glance (or two) at one's bank account.

How do wedding budgets break down? Who is responsible for covering which expenses? Will traditions help in the realm of modern cash flow? Weddings can create financial black holes for all participants, and one must be aware of the pitfalls.

Traditional Basics

Traditional etiquette is fascinating in the way it breaks down primary expenses, assigning them alternately to the bride's family and the groom (generally not indicating that his family should share the burden). The reasoning behind placing the bulk of the wedding burden on the bride's family is that the bride was considered a child, a creature under her father's protection, until he gave her to her husband at the altar and as a result she became her husband's responsibility. Does it go without saying that this attitude no longer makes much sense?

The Bride/Bride's Family Traditionally Pays For

- Printed invitations and announcements, enclosures, any other stationery, postage
- The bride's wedding dress (or outfit) and occasionally the attendants' dresses as well, if it is financially feasible (The latter may be a holdover from the United Kingdom, where it is not uncommon for the bride to foot the bill for her attendants' attire.)
- Wedding planner (if necessary or desired)
- All reception expenses
- Flowers for the wedding location, reception location, bride's family (corsages, boutonnieres, attendant bouquets), and *usually* the bride's bouquet (though occasionally, the groom pays for this one floral item)
- Bridal and household trousseaus (Stop laughing, I said it was *traditional*. This includes clothing for the bride's new life as a grown-up woman as well as a host of household linens, and occasionally china and silverware. Most of these items have turned into wedding presents and now appear on registries.)
- The groom's wedding ring (unless, of course, he isn't going to wear one)

- Officiant fee or donation if he or she is affiliated with the bride's side
- Transportation and accommodation for the officiant if he or she is affiliated with the bride's side
- Wedding photographs (and videography or other means of documenting the event)
- Music for the wedding and reception
- Transportation to and from the wedding site and reception
- Presents for the bridal attendants
- Accommodation for all bridal attendants who have come in from out of town and who can't be put up with relatives or friends (unless this is prohibitively expensive)
- Wedding present for the groom (if desired)
- Prewedding "Bridesmaids' Luncheon," if one is desired

The Groom/Groom's Family Traditionally Pays For

- The marriage license
- The bride's engagement ring
- The bride's wedding ring
- The rehearsal dinner
- Flowers: corsages and boutonnieres for the groom's family and attendants, and *occasionally* the bride's bouquet (These expenses are sometimes absorbed into the bride's larger floral plans.)
- Accessories for the groom's attendants if they did not have or rent them already (ties, gloves, etc.)
- Officiant fee or donation if he or she is affiliated with the groom's side
- Transportation and accommodation for the officiant if he or she is affiliated with the groom's family

- Presents for the groom's attendants
- Accommodation for all groom's attendants who have come in from out of town and who can't be put up with relatives and friends (unless this is prohibitively expensive)
- Bachelor dinner
- Transportation for groom's parents to and from the wedding and reception sites
- Wedding present for the bride (if desired)
- Honeymoon expenses
- House and furnishings to live in after the wedding (See? What did I say about this being the most traditional breakdown of expenses?)

Bride's Attendants' Expenses

- Clothing and accessories for the wedding (unless the bride's family is footing the bill—a rarity)
- Transportation to and from the wedding
- Contribution to the bridesmaids' group wedding present to the bride (very traditional)
- Individual wedding present for the wedding couple
- Contribution to the shower for the bride

Groom's Attendants' Expenses

- Wedding attire rental or purchase
- Transportation to and from the wedding
- Contribution to the groom's party's group present to the groom (very traditional)
- Individual wedding present for the wedding couple

- If the groom does not plan his own bachelor dinner, the groomsmen collectively pay for it. (Note the language does not refer to a bachelor *party*. Not surprisingly, bachelor parties fall somewhat outside the umbrella of traditional etiquette.)

Twisting Tradition

Does that breakdown look odd? It should, since it is predicated on a more than antiquated notion of familial responsibility, masculine solvency, and feminine dependence. Roll your eyes, if you like, but don't bypass these lists. It is worth examining them to see what people may be thinking and what the general expenses are. Almost every wedding magazine you pick up contains pullout budget worksheets (a seriously different kind of centerfold from the norm, and one that conjures very different fantasies), but these are useful only once you've sorted out the big picture.

There is no single contemporary protocol for wedding budgets, but there are a number of strategies that brides, grooms, their parents, and the members of their wedding parties can employ to make sense of nuptial financial commitments. These can help everyone find a degree of peace, if not total satisfaction.

Take Charge

If you want to maintain the greatest amount of control over your nuptials, the choice is simple: pay for everything yourselves. There are upsides and downsides to this decision. You may not be able to finance your dream wedding, but being in charge of the purse strings means your opinion carries the most weight. This doesn't mean you will have free rein to ignore anyone's requests.

Keep in mind that many suggestions will be pouring in from your relatives and future in-laws. Rampantly dismissing them may bring temporary triumph, but there is a good chance that postnuptial complaints, both passive and aggressive, will show up to make holidays sour for years to come. Compromise is a trade-off for accepting money from other people, but it is also often a trade-off for having an engaged and interested family, so take care before you put your foot down too hard on every issue.

Wheeling and Dealing

Make no mistake: The wedding cash factor has as much to do with psychology as it does with practicality. When parents feel they have some control over how their money gets spent, they are less likely to feel that they have been ignored or taken advantage of, and if the bride and groom decide to collaborate with the parents who are contributing, they won't feel guilty or worry that their own nuptial fantasies are being dashed.

Figuring out how to collaborate requires openness and tact. If parents would like to contribute financially and creatively to the nuptials, they should announce their willingness to their children. In return, the bride and groom should not simply nod and hold out open palms, expecting a pile of checks. They should prepare themselves by coming up with a list of wedding elements over which they wouldn't mind their parents (or other interested parties) having creative influence. Then they could say, "Thank you. That's very generous. Would you like to help out with the location, food, the dress, or the photographs?"

The key to making this work is for the bride and groom to accept input on things they feel flexible about. If a bride has already decided that she must have a lemon poppy-seed wedding cake and nothing else because this is the cake she and her fiancé shared on their first date together, then this is not the issue on which to request parental input. On the other hand, if a set of parents feels very strongly about photography and the bride and groom only care enough to want some sort of record of the wedding, then this is the perfect opportunity to make parents feel happy, included, and satisfied that they aren't paying for stuff they hate.

Even When You Don't Write the Checks . . . You Still Pay

While it isn't a given that the bride's family will foot the bill for the bulk of the wedding, the tradition isn't entirely dead. It is also far from unheard of for the groom's family to pay for the wedding (though this was something that was strongly frowned upon through the mid-twentieth century). Whether you are the beneficiary of such generosity or the person with the open wallet, keep a thing or two in mind.

The fact that others are paying your bills doesn't give you license to exclude or exploit your benefactors. It is critical that you be sensitive to their interests. While this doesn't mean caving to their every whim, you should not be dismissive or bratty. If they are paying, the chances are high that they'll want their tastes reflected on the invitation, their say in the guest list, and a hand in planning the reception menu. Their fingerprints will very likely be all over your nuptials, and they deserve to have them there. When you accept cash, you usually also have to accept that the people who come with it have feelings and opinions.

The way to handle parental requests (or demands) is to be open and prepared to negotiate. If you are vegetarian, but your parents urge you to serve a meat course, consider a carnivore option on your reception menu, or start wheeling and dealing. In this example, you could conjure a list of vegetarian dishes that won't confuse or intimidate people with more limited, less imaginative palates and suggest those choices to your parents. Digging in your heels or getting angry about your beliefs or social commitments (no matter how virtuous or reasonable they are) will be like waving a red cape in front of your benefactors. Be diplomatic and respectful, and if you can't get everything you want, perhaps you can get them to meet you halfway.

Contrariwise, if you are a parent and are paying for all or part of the wedding, do not confuse this event with your own nuptials. This is not the time to embrace your inner dictator and expect the bride and groom to be living dolls that you will dress up to your taste and exhibit in a setting that you decorated, eating only food you selected, in front of a crowd composed exclusively of your friends and family. A wedding is an enormous step toward adulthood (if the bride and groom haven't crossed that threshold already), and as grown-ups, the wedding couple will want to exercise some choice. Allow this, but don't be a doormat. Know when you need to draw a financial or emotional line and be ready to go back and forth a bit on some decisions. No one has to "win" anything. You're planning a fabulous party, so look for ways to make everyone happy, not sullen.

A Fistful of Dollars

Another option that appeals to parents who want to participate but who don't want to make decisions or negotiate or plan or even think excessively about wedding planning is for them to give their children some money to be spent on the wedding. This offer should not come with rules or restrictions ("I'm taking my money back if you wear a strapless dress/show off that horrible tattoo/invite that revolting woman your brother married/skip the full Catholic mass/serve that weird vegan food/etc."). It should come from a place of benevolent detachment. You are loving and invested, but not really interested in wedding minutiae.

If you're getting married and you get a big check with orders to spend the money on your wedding, rejoice, but don't think this money comes without strings or take this as a sign of your parents' disinterest. Keep them in the loop on big decisions. Invitations, for instance, can cause all kinds of trouble. Whether they've contributed lots of money or only emotional support, parents will want to at least know what you're planning on having the invitations say, so don't just print them up and send them out hoping no one will notice what's written on them. Be brave, give the parents a chance to argue with you, and be ready either to make your case or compromise. (Invitation politics, by the way, are discussed at length in chapter 8, "In Print: Wedding Stationery and What to Write on It.")

Innocent Bystanders: The Wedding Party and Guests

No one—not the groom, not the guests, not the mother of the bride—escapes having to wrestle with some financial considerations when it comes to weddings. The bottom line is this: *Everyone has financial obligations that go beyond merely attending the wedding.* Warn your wedding party about what you expect them to buy (dress, tuxedo, hair extensions, whatever) or do (throw a shower, pitch a bachelor party in Las Vegas) and give them a chance to opt out if they're strapped for cash. Let your guests know your wedding details early so they can start to gauge transportation and accommodation expenses and vacation time. Do not be offended if people are unable to attend or be in the wedding party because of financial limitations. If you suddenly realize you can't pay for your daughter's dream cake, offer to pay for something less splendid. If you're a maid of honor planning a fancy country club bridal shower for your friend, consult with the rest of the wedding party to see if they can afford their share of the fees, and be prepared to come up with other ideas. Those are the breaks. Everyone needs to be honest and graceful. If you can't afford it, don't do it, but be gentle and kind. There's no shame in being conscious of your finances.

====== *Etiquette in Action* ======

DO WE PAY?

Dear Elise,

Our daughter and her boyfriend are eloping. Are we expected to pay for their plane fare, ceremony, and hotel room?

—Daughter's Getting Hitched

Dear DGH,

Your question is simple, but my mind reels with queries. Did you offer to host your daughter's wedding? Are you planning on attending the event? Did she announce plans to elope, leaving you wondering if you have any role to play in the wedding? Do you *want* to pay for the flights, ceremony, and accommodations?

You are the author of whatever financial expectations your daughter can reasonably have of you. She may have all kinds of wishes, but unless you have promised something, there are no expectations you have to meet. You can, of course, offer to foot all or part of the bills, but you don't have to pay for this elopement. There is no imperative at all. There never is, really.

CAN'T DO IT ALL

Dear Elise,

I have had my last few summers completely booked up with weddings and wedding events. I have been a bridesmaid multiple times and traveled out of the country and to several states to attend all of the events. This has been expensive and time-consuming.

Next year I will probably be invited to ten weddings, and one of the brides just asked me to be a bridesmaid. I am honored and flattered, but my boyfriend and I just got engaged and I'm overwhelmed at the prospect of being a bridesmaid again, since I'm going to be devoting a lot of time and money toward my own wedding in the coming months. Is it rude of me to decline the invitation to be a bridesmaid?

—Wants Harmony

Dear WH,

Even if you didn't have ten other weddings to attend on top of planning your own, you wouldn't have to worry about being rude for declining the honor of being a bridesmaid. In fact, being up-front about your limits demonstrates your respect for the friend who is getting married.

The title of bridesmaid is hardly one you can't refuse. It feels uncomfortable, of course, because the bride is a friend and offering you a position of honor in her wedding. Really, though, "bridesmaid" is a job, and everyone will be happiest if you treat the position professionally. If you can't handle the workload, and the (financial or temporal) obligations, then you are absolutely right to bow out. Tell your friend that you are flattered and touched that she thought of you, and in any other year you would jump at the chance to be in her wedding, but between planning your wedding and respecting your other obligations, you can't take on so much responsibility. You can offer to take on a role in the wedding that has fewer obligations (as a reader in the ceremony, for instance), or you can offer to help in some other, less momentous, capacity.

Keep in mind that how you handle this situation depends on what sort of relationship you have with the bride and what kind of wedding she is having. If the bride is a family member or in-law, it might be harder, and less desirable in the long run, to back out entirely. If the bride is a more distant friend who is having a large wedding party, your absence is less likely to hurt her if you continue to be supportive and caring. If, on the other hand, she is a close friend who is interested in having only two bridesmaids, you being one of them, and she doesn't have hugely expensive expectations of you, then you may want to rethink turning her down. With these decisions, it is important to think about the future.

WHO PAYS?

Dear Elise,

A friend asked me to attend his relative's out-of-state wedding as his date. Whose responsibility is it to pay for my flight?

—Expenses Paid?

Dear Expenses,

The whole question of whether or not to go dutch on dates has been made murky over the ages. People are always ready to turn this into a question of feminism or capitalism, age or beauty, privilege or commerce.

In all fairness, your friend should pay for your ticket. He is inviting you to this wedding as his date and should assume this expense, which is substantial. This is a classic etiquette situation, where the general policy holds that the person who does the inviting pays for the invitee. This practice has rightly become rather relaxed, but your situation shows how the spirit of the tradition can still be vital.

FUTURE IN-LAWS AND BAD BUDGET BEHAVIOR

Dear Elise,

I've recently gotten engaged, and I am having trouble getting my wedding plans off the ground. Right now, my fiancé's family's guest list is three times larger than the one my fiancé and I put together. His parents say that they will pay for their guests but won't contribute any money that I might use for any of my guests or wedding expenses.

This setup makes me uncomfortable. I can't afford a reception for such a big crowd, and I don't know how to proceed with planning. My fiancé thinks the situation is fine and doesn't understand that it is impossible to plan a wedding without having a good sense of how many people will be on the guest list (I can't even start pricing things without knowing how many people we will invite). I don't have a clue as to how to begin planning in these circumstances.

What can I do to convince him that his parents are being unreasonable?

—Am I Overreacting?

Dear AIO,

You are not overreacting. Your fiancé's parents are being difficult and unrealistic. This doesn't mean that all hope is lost. It may be that they're just a little dim and don't realize what goes into planning a wedding.

Weddings are joint ventures. This makes some sense, since they represent the coming together of two families and really, people shouldn't be nickel-and-diming one another in this way, especially when one "side" is threatening to be three times larger than the other. This leaves you in an impossible situation, planning-wise, and I'm not sure how you'd even begin to select a venue, since there is quite a difference between planning (and paying for) a wedding with a guest list of, say, 30 people and one of 120.

Try to get your fiancé to see your perspective. Give him an opportunity to call a few venues and see how far he gets in determining what the cost is when he's pricing an event with a guest list of 30, knowing that another 90 people could also be invited. He won't even be able to determine the size of a venue to book, let alone how much of a budget he has to work with.

If he remains firm that his parents' plan is correct, take a different path. Explain that since you can't plan under those circumstances, you'd prefer to get married at city hall and have a small dinner afterward. Tell him you'll invite as many people as you can afford, and that if his parents want to throw a groom's-side-only reception some other time, that's fine with you.

You'll never win this by fighting about it. Your fiancé's parents have dug in, and your fiancé is either afraid of them or unwilling to see another perspective. The only other tactics would be to disengage or turn the tables on your future in-laws and abdicate control by saying that you are happy to contribute a fixed sum to the wedding for your guests, and they can plan accordingly.

It is a shame you're in such a spot, and I hope your fiancé comes around and figures out how to side with you over his parents, because it is an unpleasant thing to have to start married life with a couple of people and their calculator sitting on your shoulders.

Chapter 3

Bridesmaidland: The Wedding Party and Its Discontents

Are there any other moments in an adult's life where one picks certain friends, dresses them similarly, and holds them up in front of an audience as if to say, "I like these people better than all of you"? It's a unique situation, and one that's bound to inspire some ire.

Welcome to Bridesmaidland, where despite everyone's best intentions, anything can, and will, go wrong. Who knows why? Maybe the abrupt intimacy that comes with being made part of someone's wedding fantasies breeds distaste. Bride and groom, parents and siblings, best friends of all sexes, and even small children have the potential to crack under the intense obligation and heightened emotions that being a member of a wedding party causes.

Whether you love tradition or think the standard path is only for people with tiny imaginations and bottomless pockets, knowing the rules will help you minimize the damage, spare everyone's feelings, and keep friendships from going to hell. Here, maybe more than in any other area of wedding planning, it is important to be sensitive, even about etiquette. Remember, etiquette is not about keeping score to see how many times the bride screws up, or counting the ways the wedding party fails in its missions. It's about keeping the peace.

Traditional Basics

Everyone has a bridesmaid war story—either her own or someone else's—sitting in her mental vault, ready to be told when cocktail-party chatter gets slow. These tales are the stuff of legends and nightmares. Interestingly, they are also the product of a lot of contemporary interpretations of what is traditional that may or may not have anything to do with actual standards of etiquette.

To clear the air, here are the standard policies for the whole wedding party, since while bridesmaids tend to suffer the most, the rest of the wedding party isn't immune to wedding excesses.

The Setup

Traditional wedding parties are two-sided. The bride's side can have:

- maid (and/or matron) of honor
- bridesmaid(s)
- junior bridesmaid(s)
- flower girl(s)

The groom's side can have:

- best man
- groomsmen (a.k.a. ushers)
- ring bearer

There is no ideal wedding party size, and the bride's and groom's sides do not have to match. The key to determining how many wedding attendants is too many is whether or not you can pronounce the number with a straight face.

The Bride's Side

The *maid* or *matron of honor* is traditionally the bride's sister, but can also be another relative or close friend. "Matron" is the title used if the woman in question is or has ever been married. Wedding parties can have both a maid and a matron of honor.

Standard maid of honor duties include negotiating parties (bridal shower, bachelorette) with the bride and the bridesmaids; determining whether the bridal party will give a collective wedding present, collecting money for it, and purchasing it; attending the rehearsal and rehearsal dinner; being responsible for the groom's wedding ring; taking part in the wedding ceremony; and signing the marriage license as the bride's witness.

Bridesmaids are typically close friends and relatives of the bride, though there is some tradition in including the groom's sisters in the bridal party.

Bridal party duties include organizing and throwing the two big bride-oriented parties—the wedding shower and the bachelorette party. Members of the bridal party support the bride and help her with her reasonable projects. Bridesmaids go to the rehearsal and rehearsal dinner. Needless to say, they participate in the wedding and occasionally sing or give readings. The bridal party also traditionally goes in on a wedding present for the bride and groom.

Junior bridesmaid is a stopgap position for girls who are too old to be flower girls and too young to have a driver's license. It is really an honor role, and all they should be expected to do is acquire the dress and attend the rehearsal and the wedding itself.

Flower girls are often the children of close relatives (or even the bride or groom themselves). They need not be girls. They are only required to look adorable and walk in the processional, often throwing flower petals as they go. Any mistakes they make are considered charming and can be used as amusing icebreakers at the reception. Having said that, it is in everyone's best interests to walk children through the ceremony at the wedding rehearsal. (Traditionally, their presence is not required at the rehearsal dinner.)

The Groom's Side

The *best man* is the maid of honor's opposite number. This role is played by the groom's brother or another male relative or friend.

Traditional best man tasks include organizing the bachelor party if there is one; going to the rehearsal and rehearsal dinner; being responsible for the wedding ring before and during the ceremony (if there is a ring bearer, the best man makes sure that the ring is where it needs to be); taking part in the ceremony; signing the marriage license as the groom's witness; and giving the first toast at the wedding reception.

Groomsmen, a.k.a. *ushers*, help seat guests at church weddings. Like bridesmaids, they are either close friends or relatives of the groom. If there is no need to seat guests, they will form part of the processional and stand on the groom's side. This is the crowd that is most likely to plan and attend the bachelor party, if there is one. They attend the rehearsal and rehearsal dinner and traditionally get a group present for the bride and groom.

The *ring bearer* is usually a boy. He carries the wedding ring (or rings) on a pillow or on his person as part of the procession to the altar and gives them to the groom and bride at the appropriate moment. He should attend the rehearsal (though, as is the case with flower girls, not necessarily the rehearsal dinner).

The ring bearer does not *have to* actually carry the rings. He can simply walk down the aisle with the pillow as a ceremonial gesture while a more responsible adult carries the ring or rings.

Costs, Rituals, and Other Obligations

Wedding party attire is chosen by the bride and groom. As a general matter, all members of the wedding party purchase the clothes they will wear to the wedding (bridesmaid dress, tuxedo, suit, flower girl dress, etc.) and accessories (shoes, undergarments, hairstyling, makeup). There are some exceptions (if the party is lucky!) and regional traditions where the bride's family pays for the bridesmaid dresses.

Travel expenses are also the responsibility of each member of the wedding party.

Accommodations are traditionally taken care of by the wedding couple. However, if the bride and groom can't afford to put up the entire out-of-town contingent of the wedding party, or find friends or relatives with whom they can stay gratis, everyone should be prepared put him- or herself up.

Small thank-you presents are given to each member of the wedding party by the bride and groom.

Toasts at the rehearsal dinner and/or wedding reception are typically given by some members of the wedding party, particularly the best man.

Twisting Tradition

There are plenty of ways that brides, grooms, parents, and prospective attendants can bag the typical "been there, done that" wedding party routine without everyone around them assuming they've lost their minds.

Skip It

Opting out is a luxury in which more people should feel comfortable indulging. Not having a bridal party saves time and money, and it spares everyone's feelings in endless ways. Selecting members of a wedding party is an uncomfortable construct to begin with. In their earliest pagan incarnations, bridesmaids were nuptial sacrificial lambs. They were supposed to be pretty decoys that surrounded the bride so that rival suitors or highwaymen or wicked fairies would spirit away one of the friends instead of the star attraction. Given that background, what kind of an honor is it really to be a bridesmaid?

Think of the things no one will be able to say to you if you don't have a bridal party: "This bridesmaid dress makes me look fat!" "Why can't my daughter be a flower girl?" "No one told me I was supposed to rent a tux!" "If I can't be your maid of honor, I'm not coming!" "Why can't my husband be an usher?" Instead, the only big question you'll be hit with is: "Why aren't you having a wedding party?" and this is the handy answer that will blossom from your lips: "I love so many people, I didn't want to have to choose which ones I like best."

Think Small

Wedding parties are not all-or-nothing deals. Brides and grooms can opt to have only a maid of honor and best man or even a single relative standing up with them. Tiny bridal parties are almost as good as nonexistent ones for cutting short any complaints or arguments people might make about wanting to be included. They can also be an uncomplicated and elegant way to honor any children the bride and groom had before they decided to get married.

Men and Women Cross the Aisle

Women, if your closest friend and most trusted companion is your brother, there is no reason to slot some "also-ran" into the maid of honor position. Men, if your best friend is a woman you've known since kindergarten, she can be your "best man." It is happier to make the job non-gender-discriminating than it is to have someone less than ideal standing at your side. This also applies to bridesmaids, groomsmen, flower girls, and ring bearers. Of course appearances matter. If they weren't important, you might not be having a bridal party in the first place. But it is better to be surrounded by the people you actually care about, not just the ones who will generate the most palatable wedding pictures. It's your wedding, not a magazine spread.

Of course, having coed bridesmaids or groomsmen means that everyone needs to let go of notions of matching outfits (unless your friends have a penchant for cross-dressing and are actually good at it), and titles on programs should be replaced with something gender-neutral. Each sex is perfectly capable of playing a part on either side of the aisle, with the possible exception of bachelor/bachelorette party planning, but if you are determined to have a dark night on the town, anyone can step in and organize it. Plot it yourself, for that matter.

Mom of Honor? Best Dad?

While it's actually entirely keeping with tradition, people still wonder about whether they can cast parents in the roles of best man or matron of honor.

They can. It is a safe choice that no one can quibble about, and if you are fortunate enough to be so close to your parents, you should celebrate it. If you invite a parent to join the wedding party and he or she balks, you can point out that having parents in the bridal party is a tradition so old that it is becoming new again.

What's Wrong with Four Feet?

They live with you, they let you cry on them, and they have stuck by you in times high and low. Why not include your pet in your wedding ceremony?

Since the world can be divided into people who love animals and people who don't, especially in a formal setting, brace yourself for potential arguments if people in positions of authority (parents, generally speaking) object to alternate-species honor attendants. The best way to counter the argument that having a dog (or cat or ferret or tiny pony) as best man is tantamount to walking down the aisle dangling a teddy bear by the arm is to assume an adult posture. Calmly say that your decision makes you happy. Explain that you've already gotten permission from the venue to bring your pet to the ceremony and you've made arrangements for him or her to be taken care of, so there will be no chance of accidents or unhappiness—animal or human.

Looks Matter: Matchy Smatchy

Bridesmaids don't have to match. Just knowing that the whole history of look-alike attendants comes from a superstition involving human sacrifice should be enough to make you skeptical. Add to this the fact that it is difficult to find a single style that flatters multiple body types and you'll find there is something liberating about not forcing your friends to buy matching dresses. (This is less of an issue for men, who tend to have more flexibility—they either wear their own suits or rent ones that require only a quick fitting.)

If you still want your bridesmaids to have a consistent "look," you can pick a fabric and let your attendants deal with the style, or choose a color and tell your friends to figure things out for themselves. If you are really concerned that people should be able to identify your attendants quickly and easily, you can give them all coordinating bouquets, but the fact that they will be participating in the wedding procession will clear up any mystery about who's standing up for you.

Looks Matter: *What to Do About That Tattoo*

If your best friend, the bride, asks you to spackle concealer over your Celtic knot tattoos, should you tender your resignation as bridesmaid? What if your maid of honor shaves her head a few short weeks before the big day? First, put your claws away and give your friend the benefit of the doubt. Chances are the bride is only troubled by the tattoo because her grandmother keeps bringing it up, and the bridesmaid wasn't thinking about the wedding when she got the chop.

Bottom line: For everyone but the bride and groom, the wedding is an isolated event. While it is fair for the wedding couple to ask their friends to wear special clothes or put on a little makeup, it is beyond the pale to demand that they do anything that can't be undone in ten minutes with some soap and water or nail polish remover. The opposite is also true. If the bride or groom asks that someone cover up a tattoo or hide a piercing for a few hours, for whatever reason, it isn't that much more unreasonable than having to buy a dress or find a tuxedo. Weddings are defined by compromise, so everyone needs to be prepared to stifle self-expression for a few hours. Once the hangover wears

off the morning after, no one will remember what the bride'
like or whether she had a bleeding heart tattooed on her fore.
easier just to accommodate in small ways? If it is too much to ask, let i.
general matter, no one will accuse a bridesmaid of bad taste if the bride pick.
hideous bridesmaid dress, but conversely, no one can criticize the bride for her
friend's body modifications.

Combating Disapproval

You'll face it in weird places and unexpected ways. Once your wedding party
is all set, a parent will frown and ask why you haven't asked your cousin, or
your soon-to-be mother-in-law wonders why your future sister-in-law has been
denied a position of honor. Perhaps your matron of honor thinks one of your
bridesmaids is too hairy for the job, or doesn't like the kid you've picked to be
the flower girl. All of a sudden you're back in middle school having to defend
your friends and unconventional choices.

Of course you want to tell them all to go to hell and leave you alone. But
pause. There is a chance you can make this work for you. Be flexible without
being a pushover and adopt a wartime mentality. Would it be strategically wise
to include a future sibling-in-law in the wedding party? Consider how smugly
above the fray you can be come holiday time when everyone is trotting out real
and imagined slights to make the season bitter. On the other hand, why should
you cave to include someone you actively dislike or fire someone you love just
to please someone else who is overly invested in your nuptials? Weigh your
options; sometimes being inclusive offers great future rewards.

If you decide to stand your ground, do not fight. Master this phrase: "I
understand your feelings, but I really can't change my plans. I'm sorry." Repeat
it and variations of it as many times as you have to. Since you'll never be able to

convince anyone who is set on changing your wedding party that you're doing the right thing, explanations are useless. Listen, smile sweetly, and dig in your heels.

Thanks, But No Thanks

Everyone's been in a one-sided relationship, and there's nothing like a wedding party to reveal unrequited friendships. Words to the wise, brides and grooms: If you don't want someone in your bridal party, do not make the invitation—you'll only resent being bullied and possibly end up hurting your friend's feelings more than you would have by leaving him or her out. Friends and relatives: If you really don't want to be in the wedding party, gently beg off.

How can you reject someone gracefully? Resist complicated explanations. Brides and grooms should simply say that, as flattered as you are that your friend wants to join the wedding party, you've made your decisions and can't change your mind now. Do not offer your friend a consolation honorific—nothing shouts "I don't like you very much" quite as loudly as offering him or her a "guest book attendant" position. Potential bridal party members who would rather not accept this mission have a little more explaining to do. Acknowledge the honor, but say that you don't have the resources (which can be time or money—preferably not both, because piling on the excuses rings false, even if they're true) to do the job well. Be kind and interested and offer support as a civilian.

Some offers you really can refuse.

You're Fired!

Can you fire a bridesmaid or groomsman without fallout? Anything is possible, but it is highly unlikely. This is one of those gestures that, once made, is almost impossible to forget. Even if the person you oust is thrilled to be off the hook, the rejection will still sting.

How do you do it? First, make sure you know what you're doing. This gesture may terminate your friendship. Don't be frivolous. Be sure you want to cut your friend (or former friend) from the wedding lineup, and be sure your reasons are reasonable, so you don't do anything you come to regret. It is shortsighted and nasty to fire attendants for stupid reasons, such as pregnancy, weight gain, weight loss, bad teeth, a hectic schedule, bad taste in men, sick kids, or lack of slavish devotion to you and your wedding.

Once you've made up your mind, be quick about it. Don't wait until after your soon-to-be ex-friend has participated in a shower or bought a dress. (If it's too late, and a dress has been purchased or tuxedo rented, then the only gracious thing to do is offer to reimburse expenses.) Sit down and explain your decision. Remain calm but firm and, if things haven't gotten too unpleasant, insist that the former bridal attendant is welcome to be a "civilian" guest. This is the Pollyanna view of how things will go. It is unlikely you'll have much to do with each other ever again. Word to the wise: Don't eject family members (or future family members) from the wedding party, except in circumstances of real threat and abuse, unless you cherish a future of horrific holidays and spite.

I Quit!

Members of the wedding party have slightly more luck extracting themselves from their positions without destroying friendships. This doesn't mean you should just drop out the second you feel inconvenienced. Among the bad reasons for quitting the wedding party are: don't like the dress; bride doesn't call you enough; boyfriend of three weeks wants to go to Bora Bora; not so much in the mood anymore; groom wants a day of golf instead of a night with lap dancing; bride didn't invite your wife to be a bridesmaid but you're the best man.

But if you are overwhelmed and misused, you can either negotiate for fewer duties or extract yourself completely. Tell your friend that while you really appreciate the honor, your circumstances won't allow you to keep up with your duties, and rather than be a burden or generate resentment, you think it would be best to step down. Take action as soon as you are sure you can't be in the wedding, so that your friends have enough time to restructure their plans and aren't (more) freaked out right before their wedding.

I'm Against It

It is an unfortunate but reliable truth that friends won't choose the people to marry that you would pick for them. This can leave prospective members of the wedding party with some hard choices if they truly can't support a marriage. Is it worth possibly losing a friendship in the name of not being able to rejoice in the union? That is a completely individual decision and has as much to do with the belief that one is standing up in support of a friend (for better or worse) as it does with the feeling that one is approving of the marriage. It is not hypocritical or sinful to be in a wedding party if you have no faith in the wedding—or in marriage generally, for that matter. The harshness comes from abandoning a friend at a moment when he or she needs support. Think of it this way: If the marriage doesn't work out, you'll be in a position to help your friend as long as you don't say something annoying like "I knew it wouldn't last."

===========   *Etiquette in Action*   ===========

BRIDESMAID DRESS GOES ANOTHER ROUND

Dear Elise,

I'm thinking about asking one of my girlfriends if I can have my bridesmaids use the bridesmaid dresses she had us wear at her wedding. We have always had similar tastes, and our bridesmaids overlap. What would be the best way to go about asking her?

—Sassy Saver

Dear Sassy,

Hypersensitivity runs rampant when it comes to bridesmaids. Tread lightly and be prepared to have to pick new dresses. Your friend will either be flattered that you like the dresses she picked enough to include them in your wedding and pleased that everyone can save some money—or turned off.

Take stock of the dress and imagine how it would look in the context of your wedding. Many women feel anxious about friends (and relatives) copying their wedding plans, so reassure your friend that you will do your best not to recall her nuptials when you repurpose the dresses.

It would be wonderful if your friend goes along with this scheme. The expenses of being a bridesmaid can really try friendships, but be sure to give yourself time to come up with a new plan if your friend resists your idea.

AN ENEMY ON THE INSIDE

Dear Elise,

I just found out that my future sister-in-law does not care for me. Before this happened, I asked her to be an attendant in my wedding. Now I would prefer if she weren't. How do I handle this?

—Confused

Dear Confused,

Before you do anything, consider the consequences. The sister is family. If you kick her out of your wedding party, you'll still have to encounter her at events for ages to come. Are you prepared for years of discomfort, spiteful glances across punch bowls, awkward seating arrangements at Thanksgiving dinners, and sniping over birthday cake? Firing her could be eternally nasty.

Very few wedding parties are enhanced by the presence of a sourpuss, so you may be able to offer her an out. You or your fiancé could ask her directly if, given her feelings, she would be more comfortable with a different role in the wedding, or none at all. You'd have to be careful and reassure her that everyone's comfort is your primary concern. You will be best served by being, paradoxically, open and indirect at the same time. Allow her to feel that she is making the decision either to bow out or buck up.

ATTENDANT ACCOMMODATIONS

Dear Elise,

I just heard that it is customary for the bride to pay for the maid of honor's hotel if she is coming from out of town. Is this true?

—No Vacancies

Dear No Vacancies,

The bind you find yourself in is that the answer to your question is both yes and no. Traditionally, it is considered the responsibility of the bride's side to assume the accommodation expenses for all the members of the bridal party (the groom's side historically pays for the groomsmen's hotel rooms). Alternatively, each side finds free lodging for the wedding attendants with local friends and family. The maid of honor is not alone in enjoying this favor.

This can be an expensive proposition, but one that must be handled fairly. If the bride offers to house or purchase lodging for one, she must make the gesture universal. If she can't afford to do this and can't put them all up with friends, she could try to arrange to get a discount rate on a block of hotel rooms, which would help offset the costs somewhat, while still being fair to the bunch.

ONE ODD DRESS

Dear Elise,

I have five bridesmaids for whom I bought dresses. My fiancé's cousin ordered her dress a size too small, saying she would lose weight, but she has gained weight instead. We tried to get her a larger dress, but the design has been discontinued. I have another bridesmaid who doesn't seem too interested in my wedding who has a dress in the larger size. Should I fire her so that my fiancé's cousin can be in the bridal party? Is there any right way to handle this?

—Dress Disaster

Dear Dress Disaster,

These dresses are a trap for you. Nowhere is it written that the bridal party must wear identical dresses. They can wear similar dresses, different dresses made out of the same fabric, clothes made of different fabric in the same color, or entirely different clothing that doesn't coordinate at all. This holds for formal weddings and informal ones.

Etiquette does not require that bridesmaids match, but it does ask that people treat one another gently. You risk much more by firing a bridesmaid you feel isn't attentive enough or another for not fitting into a dress than you do by having a not-quite-matching wedding party. Do you really want to generate all of this anger and unrest with your fiancé's family? It will linger long after your wedding.

See if the dress shop can make something similar in the same fabric for your dress-less bridesmaid. Ideally, you would not cut anyone from your bridal party, and ultimately, the dresses really don't matter. It is much more important that everyone be included and comfortable, and if that means mismatched maids, that's the way it goes.

FLOWER BOY?

Dear Elise,

I would like my five-year-old nephew to participate in my wedding. I do not, however, want a ring bearer. I asked my sister if my nephew might want to be a flower boy and walk alongside the flower girl. She said that would be great but asked if he could throw something other than petals. What is wrong with a boy handling flowers? How do I talk to her about this? I really don't want a ring bearer, but I don't want to do anything that makes my sister or my nephew uncomfortable.

—Befuddled

Dear Befuddled,

Of course it doesn't matter, in the scheme of things, what your nephew throws, but you are right to recognize that this is one of those areas of parental decision making that you might not want to question. Keep in mind, by the way, that "flower boys" are not wildly unusual in weddings. You aren't proposing anything shocking.

Your sister didn't ask if her son could be the ring bearer, though it is a "traditional" role for young boys in wedding parties. All she asked was if her son could throw something other than flower petals. Would you be willing to have him toss some leaves or other light greenery, for instance? That might be a sufficiently masculine thing to do that he won't be teased about if the word of his "job" gets out. Alternatively, you could just have him escort the flower girl, throwing nothing.

SAYING NO TO MOTHER

Dear Elise,

My mother is getting remarried and asked me to be her maid of honor. I do not want to do it and told her so, but she won't accept it.

I suspect that she really just wants to have me take care of all of the wedding details she can't be bothered with, but I am really busy with work right now and don't have time to take care of all of the guests' accommodations and run endless errands.

Do I really have to be my mother's maid of honor?

—Angry & Upset

Dear A&U,

You always have choices. You can't be forced to be your mother's maid of honor, short of having a gun put to your head. You can, however, just keep saying, "I'm sorry, but I really want to be a guest and help out where I can" over and over and over again until your mother either comes around or gets married, in which case the point will be moot.

Another option is to agree to take on the role under certain conditions. You could tell her explicitly what you absolutely will not do so that you only have to do the most crucial job that a maid of honor has to do, which is stand up with the bride. Everything else is extra. If your mother complains, tell her she can find someone else. If she calls you incessantly, turn off your phone. She can try to bully you, but you are in charge of refusing to be pushed around.

This isn't the beginning and end of it. But you do have two distinct and reasonable options, both of which require that you stand up for yourself. You can absolutely be loving and respectful of your mother while protecting your boundaries.

BAD MAID OF HONOR: TRY TALKING BEFORE FIRING

Dear Elise,

I asked a friend to be my maid of honor. (I also have a matron of honor and a bridesmaid.) My maid of honor has not been very interested in my wedding, and I wonder if I made a bad decision. I don't know what to do. My fiancé says I should just talk to her, but that is a lot harder than it sounds. I know our friendship will be over if I fire her, and I don't know if I care.

—A Saddened Bride-to-Be

Dear Saddened,

Why would it be easier to fire your maid of honor and perhaps terminate your friendship with her than it would be to talk to her about what is going on? She may be in a hideous state of mind and be relieved and comforted that you took an interest in her. She may be kind of unpleasant generally and looking for a way to drop out of your wedding party. I couldn't say, but it is certainly preferable to pursue a slightly more gentle line of questioning than it is to call her up with guns blazing, saying she's out of the wedding.

This is not to say your feelings are unreasonable. You should do what you feel, in the long run, is the right decision. If, after you've given your friend a chance to explain herself or step down on her own, you're still feeling uncomfortable and unhappy, you can tell her that you'd rather she not be in the wedding party anymore.

You feel you made a hasty decision casting this woman as your maid of honor, but you don't have to counter it with a second one. In the interests of being fair and mature, give this woman a chance to salvage your friendship. If she blows it or if you still feel awful and really don't care to know her anymore, then you can talk to her about stepping down.

SIBLINGS AND THE WEDDING PARTY

Hi Elise,

I am planning my wedding and choosing the wedding party. My fiancé decided to include his brothers and sister in the wedding party and has also decided to include a male friend. I think it would be nice if he included my two brothers in his wedding party, but he said he is closer to his friend. Can I insist that my family be involved?

—Torn

Dear Torn,

Are you saying that your fiancé has already chosen to have a wedding party that includes all of his siblings and one friend? If that is the case, then it would make sense to follow his lead and have a coed bridal party with your brothers in it.

People do this all the time, and it would be a happy tribute to your brothers to have them stand up with you at the altar. You would, of course, be able to include some of your friends (female or male) in the lineup as well, and keep in mind that it is not necessary for the bride's and groom's wedding parties to be symmetrical.

On the other hand, if you are saying that your fiancé wants you to include his sister as a bridesmaid but won't accommodate your brothers, you should have a conversation with him. Unless you are inclined to just keep your siblings on your side of the aisle, remind your fiancé that the sides don't have to match numerically, and that if you're making the gesture of including his sister on your side, he should reciprocate. The presence of your brothers in the groom's party would not mean having to jettison any of his friends, so he should just adopt a "more the merrier" approach and be happy that this is a very easy gesture that pleases a lot of people for a long time—small effort, high reward.

Chapter 4

Prenuptial Frolics: Engagement Celebrations, Bridal Showers, Bachelor Parties, and Bachelorette Bashes

For the uninitiated, the cascade of social obligations an engagement announcement triggers can be astonishing. It's as if the wedding roller coaster, once flying down the tracks, can't pause, can't stop, and won't let anyone—bride, groom, wedding party, or guests—get off for a hit of Dramamine and a breather.

Weddings can create whole seasons of events: engagement parties, showers, bachelor nights, bachelorette gatherings, teas, luncheons, cocktail bashes—you name it. These are all in addition to various dress appointments (for the bride and bridesmaids), trips to scout venues, shower planning sessions, emergency drinks to rail about all of the families, celebratory meals with the very relatives you've been complaining about, and the like. There are endless opportunities for getting together for wedding-related activities.

This doesn't mean that everyone has to be on board with all possible events. Each party is a new decision. No one needs to have (or attend) all—or any—of them if they generate too much angst. They are parties, after all; they are supposed to be amusing.

Traditional Basics

Engagement Parties

- Engagement parties are traditionally hosted by the future bride's parents (though it is not considered beyond the pale for the groom's family to throw one, especially if the bride's family is far away or unavailable).

- *Timing:* There are no specific protocols for when to throw engagement parties. They can be planned to coincide with the publication of the engagement announcement in the newspaper (if there is going to be one), they can be a surprise, or they can be planned around everyone's convenience. There should be no announcement and no party if the future bride or future groom is still married to a third party.

- The party is generally a cocktail affair or dinner.

- If the engagement is being announced at the party, there are two "official" ways of handling it: The future bride and her mother can stand at the door, with the fiancé behind them, greeting guests as they arrive and breaking the news in an informal "receiving line"; alternatively, the father of the bride can pick his moment to propose a toast to the union of his daughter and her fiancé.

- Often the party is constructed around the "surprise" revelation of the engagement.

- Engagement party guest lists include the family and close friends of the wedding couple, though the parties can also be quite large open-house-style events.

- Guests may bring presents for the wedding couple, but gift giving is not necessary (obviously, this is particularly the case if the engagement news is a surprise).

- While fun, engagement parties are not necessary.

Showers

- The original purpose of bridal showers was to throw a party at which the bride-to-be was literally "showered" with practical items that she would need in her new life as a married woman. Some traditionalists suggest that showers are useless for the bride who already "has everything," but there are many variations on the standard shower so that one can be thrown without anyone seeming greedy.

- Bridal showers are traditionally single-sex (all-female) affairs, but there can certainly be coed showers.

- They are usually held three to six weeks before the wedding.

- These parties are usually hosted by the wedding party. Close friends can also do the honors. Tradition frowns hard on mothers and other immediate relatives of brides acting as shower hosts, because it seems too mercenary for them to throw parties that require their daughters be given presents.

- Showers often have themes, which mostly have to do with what sort of presents guests should bring. Some common themes are kitchen, household linen, lingerie, recipes, "around the clock" (a mildly baffling one where each guest is told to bring a gift that corresponds with an hour of the day), and "honey-do" (where people supply presents intended to encourage the future husband—and possibly even the bride herself—to make home repairs).

- Occasionally there are auxiliary present-giving enterprises, sometimes called "wishing wells." Guests bring additional small presents that usually relate to the theme of the shower (measuring spoons, bathing luxuries, slim volumes of poetry, perhaps) and put them in a large basket, creating something like a wedding-themed Christmas stocking. These items are also sorted through during the present-opening part of the festivities.

- Because showers are parties *where guests are required to bring presents*, no one should be invited to a shower who is not invited to the wedding. There are a couple of exceptions to this policy. There can be office showers hosted by coworkers who do not expect to be invited to the nuptials; and for people who are having intimate destination weddings (with only parents or other immediate family in attendance), it is not beyond the pale to have a shower and invite people who are not invited to the wedding. (If there is going to be a reception after a destination wedding, anyone invited to the shower should be included on that guest list.)

- Shower guest lists generally comprise the close friends and family of the bride. Historically, the older generation (mothers of the bride and groom) was not always included at these parties, but there was never strict policy on this.

- In addition to eating something, it is traditional—but far from necessary—to play wedding-related games at bridal showers. These games sometimes involve gently embarrassing the bride, though they can also just be simple party games where favors are awarded to the winners.

- The one activity that defines showers is the present-opening ritual, in which the bride opens each gift and passes it around to her friends. It is useful to have someone on hand keeping a record of which guest brought which present, for future thank-you note purposes.

- Some traditionalists feel that it is unnecessary to write formal thank-you notes for bridal shower gifts—that a verbal on-the-spot thanks is sufficient. This is risky. Many people will expect a thank-you note and be miffed not to receive one.

- Showers are often surprise affairs, but anyone throwing one should know whether the bride wants one or not.

- Because of the implied greed factor, guests should be invited to as few showers as possible (no more than two), and it is generally recommended that brides really have no more than two showers (unless one is thrown in a workplace setting or far away from the others, in the bride's hometown if she has moved away, for instance).

Bachelor Dinners/Bachelor Parties

- The bachelor dinner is generally held a couple of nights before the wedding.
- The event is hosted either by the groom's father (this is the traditional *bachelor dinner*, remember, not a bachelor party) or the best man and is often held in a private room or club.
- The events of the evening consist of eating, toasts, and the groom's presentation of gifts to his groomsmen. A bit of ancient tradition that disappeared sometime during the 1950s had the party hold a toast to the bride with champagne, after which each man would snap his glass's stem.
- Standard etiquette texts avoid the topic of the bachelor party entirely— surprise, surprise. Perhaps this is because the bachelor party, almost by definition, is predicated on the notion that all forms of civility and so-called "proper" behavior will be pitched out the window and not retrieved until the following morning, in between enormous quantities of analgesics, long showers, and soft lighting.

Bridesmaids' Luncheon/Bachelorette Party

- The bridesmaids' luncheon is generally scheduled a day or so before the wedding, when the bridesmaids are all in town and available.
- It is a simple party hosted by the bride's wedding attendants, and it doesn't even have to be a lunch. Everyone can gather for tea, dinner, cocktails, or brunch, if those times are more amusing or convenient.

- This is an opportune moment for the bride to give her wedding party their presents, and if the bridal party is giving a collective wedding present to the bride, now is as good a time as any to give it to her.
- Since the bachelor party goes largely unmentioned in the annals of traditional etiquette, it is even less surprising that the much more recent development of the bachelorette party would be ignored. Fear not and read on for the rules of etiquette pertaining to the event (yes, there are a few).

Twisting Tradition

Engagement Parties

DO YOU REALLY WANT ONE?

Even the sharpest traditionalists do not believe that an engagement party is necessary. It really isn't. If being the center of attention so early in the game makes you itchy, or if no one steps forward offering to throw one, don't feel bad; take a pass. One isn't required to spring the big news on one's friends and family in a grand way, and you may feel more comfortable spreading the word on your own, or letting the inevitable gossip mill take care of it. Consider how refreshing it will be for people to be able to whisper about happy news that is actually true.

DOES THE BRIDE'S FAMILY HAVE TO STEP UP SO SOON?

Really, anyone can throw an engagement party, even the future bride and groom themselves. The trick is to be very open about what's going on. If a friend expresses interest in hosting one and all the parents have been silent on the matter, it isn't a bad idea to give the parents a call and let them know you're thinking of accepting your friend's offer. As long as everyone has been gently forewarned, no one can legitimately complain about having his or her toes stepped on.

Occasionally (especially if the families are spread out) there are pleas to have multiple engagement parties. Much of traditional etiquette is predicated on a very old sense of how communities behave—the assumption often being that people don't move around much and marry locally. For anyone who has ever attempted the two-family Thanksgiving weekend tour, that notion is laughable. So even if the bride's parents are doing the traditional thing and hosting an engagement party, they should relax a little and not whine about the groom's family throwing another one if they want to have a celebration in their neck of the woods.

Who Gets Invited to These Things?

There is a certain vagueness in the traditional guidelines for engagement party guest lists. This is because there are really no set policies. An engagement party is a flourish, a nicety, and guest list choices will depend a lot on who is throwing the party and how close it will be to the wedding itself.

As with all wedding events, it is a good policy to invite people you will also be inviting to the wedding. Of course, the safest approach isn't always the easiest one to take. What if the engagement party is staged and planned before the bride and groom have decided a thing about their wedding? The further apart (temporally) these two events are, the less complicated and uncomfortable it will be to have people attending the engagement party and not the wedding. This is also the case if there are multiple engagement parties thrown in different parts of the country (or world). In these cases, the engagement party should be thought of as an end in itself: a celebration of the couple, not the beginning of the carnival of nuptial events.

GUEST RESPONSIBILITIES

Engagement party guests have one obligation (beyond showing up or politely declining): They must congratulate the future bride and groom and not dig up passive-aggressive ways to snark at the institution of marriage, the likelihood that theirs will fail, or the horror that each of the future mothers-in-law will pose to their children's spouses.

Guests do not need to bring presents. Anyone who implies that they are necessary is gravely mistaken and needs to be ignored. If you are moved to give a present, you can't go wrong with something consumable: wine or champagne, other food gifts, some luxurious household nicety, or something of specific interest to the bride and groom. No need to go nuts.

Showers

WHAT IF I DON'T WANT ONE?

Well, *I* certainly won't make you have a shower against your will. Bridal showers are a deeply ingrained tradition, but they truly are not for everyone. If you don't want one in any form, do not be bullied. Graciously decline. Repeat as necessary.

You are also entitled to make requests. If you just want to have everyone get together for cocktails and skip all the standard shower games, which you despise, tell your hosts and make sure they do not call the party a "shower." The moment the *S* word comes up, you're in for it. If you don't want to engage in the present-opening ritual, let your friends know. They're not mind readers, and nobody likes a sullen bride.

WHAT IF I CAN'T THROW ONE?

Say you're a bridesmaid, or a maid of honor, and you just can't host a bridal shower. Your reasons are actually important. If you are against bridal showers for political or philosophical reasons, you should let your friend, the bride, know about your quirk before you join the wedding party. This party that may seem infantile and hopelessly retro to you may have outrageous significance to the bride. Refusing to participate in a shower, if she has made it clear from the outset (when you could still bail) that she wants one, is hurtful. If you're feeling petty or jealous, put it aside for a while (you have the rest of your life to indulge these feelings) or bow out.

On the other hand, life can get in your way, and you might find yourself strung out with work or school, flooded with family strife, suffering from health issues, or strapped for cash. If this happens, do not ignore the shower. Tell the other attendants and the bride about your pressures and let them know exactly what you can do. If you are broke, ask if you can reimburse the rest of the wedding party for your share on some kind of extended payment plan. If time is your problem, see if there is anything you can do on off hours (addressing envelopes, for instance). It is much better to come clean than it is to turn into a flake.

WHO HOSTS?

Traditionalists do have a point when they state that it seems grabby for the mother or sisters of the bride to throw a party that demands that guests shower their daughter or sibling with presents. This is why the shower duties usually fall to the bride's attendants or close friends.

This is a good, safe policy, but one that can be bent a little or broken. If it is common knowledge that no one else is available or able, the mother of the bride or even the mother of the groom can host a bridal shower. This situation often arises as a result of proximity issues. Sometimes a bride will travel so that she can have a shower at home; or conversely, if she is unable to travel and is far away from her friends, her fiancé's family may step into the breech.

WHO ATTENDS?

There are times to rebel and times to toe the line, and wedding shower guest lists fall into the latter category. It's just too easy to insult people and appear greedy in these situations.

As a general matter, only invite people to the shower who will be invited to the wedding. The traditional standard exceptions are still reasonable: the workplace shower and the shower preceding a tiny destination wedding. Showers can even be thrown for preannounced elopements (which sounds like something of an oxymoron), though in the case of destination weddings or elopements, all shower guests should be invited to postwedding receptions, if there are any.

SHOWER PRESENTS 101: GIVING AND GREED

Wedding propaganda loves themes. One is encouraged to plan all aspects of a wedding according to colors or images or moods or all of the above. Bridal showers are not immune, and themes often lead to strange behavior and excesses when it comes to presents. Showers actually don't need to have themes. There's nothing wrong with having a simple party, at any time of the day or evening, that is all-women or coed . . . with presents, of course. Reasonable ones.

If faced with attending a themed shower, the best bet is to comply. Standard present concepts are easy to handle, because they either offer obvious inspiration (kitchen utensils!) or are very clear about not wanting you to spend any money (recipe showers, where guests are supposed to bring copies of favorite recipes so that they can be compiled into a patchwork cookbook, for instance).

Brides often register for showers, and while this takes much of the surprise out of things, it helps out guests who don't know what to give. (For more on registries of all kinds, see chapter 9, "Asking, Giving, and Getting: The Politics of Registries and Wedding Presents.") Guests also have the freedom to not use the registry. Regardless of convenience, it is indelicate to stuff registry information into shower invitations. Even though the party is all about presents, it just feels a bit crass, especially if a theme has been selected, which does some of the work of a registry anyway. Shower hosts can, of course, mention any and all registries when guests RSVP.

Then there is a set of alternative showers, which are actually poorly disguised fund-raisers. Beware of these. One recent phenomenon is the Jack and Jill shower and the form this party takes has incredible regional variations. Often, "Jack and Jill" simply designates a coed event, which is normal enough. In some places, however, the phrase is a weird euphemism for "benefit," where invitations come with admission tickets that prospective guests must purchase (the sale of which offsets the costs of the party, and any extra money goes to the wedding couple), and the party itself is full of games of chance that also require guests to shell out some cash. All the proceeds go to fund the bride and groom's new home.

This kind of party is a bad idea. It is beyond demanding, makes guests feel as if they're being bilked for cash, and really violates a central principle of etiquette, which is that invitations should have a single intention: to tell people that they are welcome and that their presence at a party—not the money they could offer—would enhance the celebration. Showers themselves are problematic, but at least guests have the ability to choose presents according to their means and aren't being charged an admission fee. Benefits befit charities and other worthy causes, and as much as the bride and groom think they deserve a down payment on a house or car or a fully funded honeymoon, they should still resist the urge to have a private fund-raiser.

If you live in an area where the Jack and Jill benefit shower is not only the norm but eagerly anticipated, you're still asking too much of your guests. If you buck local convention and opt for a shower that doesn't charge an entry fee, you may discover a secret wellspring of gratitude and relief amongst your friends and family.

Bachelor and Bachelorette Parties

Does the idea of even throwing the words "etiquette" and "stag (or stagette) party" in the same sentence strike you as oxymoronic? Do sex romps and shot-drinking contests seem to fall a little outside etiquette's civilizing parasol? Look deeper. Even in the jungle, there are laws.

- Many people don't want to have bachelor parties of any kind, whether the planned event is tame or unmentionable. If you don't want one, don't have one. If you're thinking of bullying someone who doesn't want a bachelor party into having one, save your money or go for a lap dance on your own time.
- It is up to brides and grooms to negotiate with each other what sorts of activities are acceptable or verboten. As long as the deals they negotiate are comfortable for both parties, anything goes, and whatever they work out is nobody else's business.
- Surprise bachelor/ette parties are not uncommon. If you want one (or if you don't), speak to the people most likely to plan one (friends, best man, maid of honor, etc.) and make your wishes known.
- If you want to plan an event of hedonistic, sexy extremes but know that the bride or groom in question doesn't want this kind of party, back away. You

won't make anyone happy by forcing strippers and penis-shaped lollipops on your friends.

- If the sexual rite of passage—like an evening with strippers—is up your alley, tell the people most likely to organize your party what you want. Very few people are actually psychic.

- Bachelor/ette parties come in many varieties. Here is a handful of popular possibilities: strip-club excursion (male or female), day of golf, bar crawl, weekend in Las Vegas, spa weekend.

- Bachelor/ette party guest lists, like those for other prewedding parties, are generally composed of wedding party members and friends who are invited to the wedding. This policy can bend a little. If the wedding is going to be extremely intimate and you explain this to your guests, you stand a good chance of not offending people if you ask them to join you for this last prenuptial party and don't invite them to the wedding. These parties are traditionally held close to the wedding, but the window in which they can be thrown is quite large, and they should be scheduled according to convenience. It is advisable, however, not to have a bachelor or bachelorette party the night before the wedding. That will only ensure that you will look and feel your absolute worst on the big day.

- Generally, the groom and bride are the guests of honor at their respective stag nights, and the rest of the guests pick up their tabs. No presents are required, but everyone tends to eat or at least drink at these parties, and various people at all kinds of establishments need tips.

========   *Etiquette in Action*   ========

Showers

RESTAURANT SHOWER: COULD GUESTS PAY?

Hi Elise,

My maid of honor and I are planning my bridal shower. Instead of the traditional shower, I would prefer to go to a restaurant and hang out with everyone. No gifts would be expected, but if some people bring them, I would open them later. My maid of honor is the "hostess," but she and I can't afford to buy meals for everyone. Would it be wrong to ask people to pay for their own food? How would we word such an invitation?

—I Prefer Lunch

Dear Lunch,

While your relaxed, no-pressure shower sounds wonderful, I have to advise against your plans. An invitation, in the most classical sense, should come with no strings attached, and a shower is already a complicated affair because it requires presents.

If you don't have enough money for a full luncheon, perhaps you could consider something different: a dessert party, tea, or cocktails. Another option is to ask around and see if you could negotiate with a restaurant for a limited menu that you and your maid of honor can afford. It is just too uncomfortable to place the financial burden (however small) on one's guests. Above all, you don't want to create a situation that leaves some guests miffed or disillusioned. It is much better to be direct and work within your means than to try to jury-rig something that could create hard feelings.

IT'S ALL FUN AND GAMES
UNTIL SOMEONE STARTS CRYING

Dear Elise,

I told my bridesmaids that I don't want games at my shower, and some of them said I have no choice. Others said they would skip them if I really don't want them, but seem to be waffling. Do brides have any input in their shower?

—No Games

Dear No Games,

Sometimes wedding showers, originally happy gestures geared toward furnishing an incipient household with necessities, calcify into hazing events, replete with stunts and embarrassing rituals, drinking games, and secret codes. If you like those types of situations, that's perfectly fine, and there is nothing wrong with you if you don't.

There is, however, something a little devilish about friends who want to torture you with exactly the sort of shower you despise. Perhaps they are just high on the idea of a so-called "traditional" shower and think you are protesting too much.

Sit down with your friends, preferably individually, and be very straight about your wishes. If there is protest, you can ask gently why you should be made uncomfortable and unhappy at a party in your honor. (That is the message; the phrasing of course is up to you.) You should not have to resort to threats, but you could always indicate that you will absent yourself once the games begin.

CAUGHT IN THE MIDDLE

Dear Elise,

I am a maid of honor, hosting a wedding shower for the bride. My friend can't stand her fiancé's mother. I think that if my friend's future mother-in-law's presence will make my friend tense and angry, she shouldn't be invited to the shower. Do I have to invite the mother of the groom?

—Maid of Honor in Need of Advice

Dear Maid of Honor in Need,

Your friend's situation is delicate, and while she and her future mother-in-law may have agreed to dislike each other, in the interests of peace it would be wise not to throw a party that gives the appearance of deliberately excluding the mother of the groom. Even if this woman would rather have a colonoscopy than attend her son's fiancée's shower, she will surely take offense if she learns that the bride's entire family has been invited and she alone has been excluded.

The best way to foster harmony is to throw a party that your friend's future mother-in-law wouldn't want to attend anyway. If there is any way you can have a shower with a guest list of "young" people—friends of the bride, and not her mother or older female relatives—you and your friend will have a lot less to worry about in terms of not bringing potential discord into an already volatile situation. Otherwise, invite her and hope she doesn't show. It is important to keep the peace.

VERY LATE SHOWER

Dear Elise,

My son got married a year ago. He and his wife are about to move into their first home together and could use a few household items. Since they never had a wedding shower, is it too late to give them one?

—Ready to Party

Dear Ready,

Indeed you are way too late. Your wedding shower window expired more than a year ago, and since a shower really is connected to the wedding in a primal way, your choice would appear odd, at best.

Another type of party, however, is perfect for your needs. I am referring here to the housewarming party. These are held at the new residence and will let your son and his wife show off their place. It isn't a formal party, but you can still send invitations and prepare the tasty treats of your choice, and there is a tradition for guests to bring presents, though there is not quite the same expectation of gifts as there is with wedding showers.

This is what your son and his wife really want, anyway. Showers provide so much temptation to offer lingerie and various unnecessary wedding-themed items, and your son and his wife are probably interested in things that are more practical, if equally charming.

SHOWERS AND SPENDING

Dear Elise,

I was recently invited to a relative's shower. What would be the proper amount of money to spend on a present?

—Shower Novice

Dear Novice,

Showers are insidious not only because they require that presents be presented, but also because they encourage comparisons among friends and relatives. All the gifts get put on stage and unwrapped in front of a captive audience. Guests, plied with tea sandwiches, squirm when they realize their offerings look shabby compared to others, or feel smug when theirs earn applause for creativity or luxury. In truth, no one should ever spend more money than he or she can afford on shower presents, and this is why there is no monetary guideline. If you're worried or at a loss for what to get, quiz your host to see if the bride has registered somewhere or has expressed any wishes. Above all, however, do not allow yourself to be bullied.

SCARY SHOWER LINEUP

Dear Elise,

I recently received an invitation to a shower for one of my husband's relatives. My husband has a huge family, and a lot of them will be getting hitched in the next few years. We are just starting out and we can't afford to purchase presents for every single shower and wedding.

What are our options? I do not want to appear cheap if I bring a small gift, but I also don't want to offend my husband's relatives by not attending.

—Overwhelmed

Dear Overwhelmed,

Well, you do, of course, have the option of not attending. This works best if you have a legitimate excuse.

But really, do you want to make a long-term plan out of figuring out how to dodge wedding shower invitations? There is nothing offensive or problematic about giving a present that is within your means.

While showers do require that you bring presents, there is no policy, no rule, no maxim of etiquette that says you have to bankrupt yourself. So if you feel you have to go, bring something that you can afford. Very few hosts would be happy to hear that their guests were scared to attend showers or parties because the prospect of the present was too intimidating.

Bachelor Parties

BACHELOR PARTY PARANOIA

Dear Elise,

My fiancé and I have decided that neither of us wants strippers or exotic dancers at our bachelorette and bachelor parties. I know that my friends are fine with this. His friends are not so trustworthy. How do we ensure that our agreement with each other is not compromised?

—Worried

Dear Worried,

Since bachelor and bachelorette parties are designed to buck good taste, and the classic activities at these events are not spoken of in polite society, it isn't surprising that traditional etiquette has little to say about stag party protocol.

So while yours isn't so much a question of etiquette, you and your fiancé can do a few things to ease your minds about these parties. First, it is a misunderstanding to think that he will be a hostage to his friends' plans. He can always leave any party that takes a turn he doesn't care for. Make sure he understands this.

Your fiancé should also have a word with his bachelor party's host so that no one can claim not to have known what he wanted— or didn't want—from his stag night. If he is still unsure about these proceedings, he could enlist the help of another friend who will be attending the party, so that he has some extra support if he decides he must take off.

Beyond that, you and your future husband can always call off all bachelor and bachelorette events, since they aren't necessary anyway.

BACHELORETTE PARTY AND FAIRNESS

Dear Elise,

A friend's bachelorette party will be a spa weekend, with only a couple of friends. I am really strapped for cash, and I can't afford to pay for all of the bride's and my expenses, but I don't feel I can back out.

I did say that one night away would be more affordable, but my friend said that she really wanted to do the whole weekend and that we wouldn't have to pay for everything. I have heard that the bride shouldn't pay for *anything*. Is it okay to pay for what I can?

—Embarrassed

Dear Embarrassed,

People choose bridesmaids and wedding party participants for all sorts of reasons, but friendship is supreme, not finances.

All parties need to be vocal about their wants and their financial abilities. The prickly cattiness that chokes friendships could be obliterated in many cases by people simply saying, early on, what they can afford, before "dream dresses" were decided upon and deluxe weekends planned. This way, no one can claim not to have been warned. It takes guts to do this. No one enjoys admitting to having financial limitations, but no one enjoys being pressured financially, either.

Talk to the bride about your situation. It is possible that she simply wants to go away with you for the weekend, doesn't care if she has to pay for it (or part of it), and that is that. More than anything, you'll serve your friend and yourself best if you communicate openly, pay for what you can, and support your friend.

PRESENT MANIA

Dear Elise,

My fiancé and I keep being invited to weddings that have multiple accompanying showers and parties, and we are getting burned out.

For one wedding we also had to attend an engagement party, a cocktail party, a coed honey-do shower, a lingerie bridal shower, two bachelorette parties, and one bachelor party (which required travel). We bought presents for *all* the showers. This is getting very expensive. How bad would it be if we didn't give a wedding present? Is it normal to have this many showers?

—I'm Not Really Cheap

Dear Not Cheap,

I hope you wrote from a reclining position with a stiff drink of something at your side. That is quite the party schedule to maintain.

There is no fixed or required set of prewedding events, but it does seem as if your friends went a bit overboard. In cases where people have multiple showers, they usually try not to overtax their friends by inviting them to only one, and they would have been smart to embrace that policy rather than exhaust you.

The CliffsNotes answer to your question is this: One is never required to give a wedding present. In your case, you have given quite a number of presents already and legitimately feel tapped out, which is probably not what your friends intended when they invited you to so many wedding events. But while your feelings are utterly justified, you might not feel comfortable acting on them. There are a lot of inexpensive but sincere gestures you could make. You could give them a card wishing them well (often, this is all people really want—acknowledgment that their friends are happy for them) or a token present (a cookbook, a few of your favorite mystery thrillers for them to read on their honeymoon, chocolates, a bottle of wine). At this point, you're in the clear. You have more than proved your friendship and, if nothing else, you deserve a break.

Chapter 5
Hitting the Road: Eloping and Destination Weddings

Eloping—even the word itself carries a little frisson of excitement. Fears of nuptial stodginess are wiped away by the romance of running off under the cloak of night to marry, against all odds, One's True Love.

The allure of the destination wedding is similarly glamorous. Tropical breezes, bare feet, that nice vacation feeling . . .

Apart from the picturesque reasons, many people seize upon the idea of eloping or throwing destination weddings for practical purposes involving various kinds of self-preservation. Depending on how you hit the road, you could easily save a lot of money, a lot of time, and a lot of heartache.

Traditional Basics

- Classic elopements occurred when either or both sets of parents of the engaged couple forbade the marriage. An elopement often carried shameful connotations. Remember the misery of the Bennet family in *Pride and Prejudice* when Lydia Bennet ran off to Scotland with Mr. Wickham? (Bear in mind, however, that elopements are not by definition "shotgun" weddings. "Shotgun" is a barely euphemistic euphemism for a wedding that is arranged in great haste because of a pregnancy. Today, so many brides are knocked up at their weddings that the term almost seems quaint.)

- Since the 1950s, the definition of eloping has been expanded to apply to people who, even if their families are overjoyed at their union, decide to get married quickly and privately, either in a courthouse or in a religious ceremony.

- Elopement clothing is traditionally rather somber. Men wear dark suits, while women wear suits or dresses of any color with some of the more predictable hemlines (tea-length, knee-length, etc.). They do not wear wedding gowns.

- Traditionally, if the bride's parents approve, they can send out formal marriage announcements in their names—as they would if they had hosted a regular wedding. (In this situation, the bride's parents are the ones telling the world of the union.) If the parents are not on board with the marriage, or if they'd just rather, the couple can send out wedding announcements themselves. The elopement announcements are the same as wedding announcements and should include the place (the city and, if appropriate, the name of the religious establishment), date, and year of the wedding. (For wedding announcement information, see chapter 8, "In Print: Wedding Stationery and What to Write on It.")

- Friends and family can send wedding presents to the eloped couple, but this gesture is made strictly according to the giver's taste and interest. The bride and groom should not expect presents.

- If they like, the bride's parents can throw a postelopement reception. These parties can be formal or informal. The invitation language usually looks something like this:

Bride's Parents' Names
request the pleasure of your company
at a reception in honor of
Bride and Groom (using their married names)
Date
Time
Place

- The traditional protocol for destination weddings is the same as that for regular domestic weddings. The destination wedding is a relatively contemporary phenomenon. As a result, the devil is in the details.

Twisting Tradition

While traveling is implied with both elopements and destination weddings, they really are very different sorts of nuptials. Elopements are very private—antisocial, in a good way—and don't necessarily require travel any farther than one's local courthouse, while destination weddings really are just weddings that happen in some remote locale that everyone needs to travel to get to.

Elopement Practicalities

There are many compelling reasons to elope. It saves enormous amounts of money, obliterates all guest list quandaries, and erases most if not all interfamily negotiations. An elopement can be a simple, happy, private event.

But with these advantages come a few necessary trade-offs.

Elopements are, by definition, not large or fancy affairs. You can't issue invitations or expect scads of presents and parties with bridesmaids and a lot of the nuptial flourishes that Wedding Culture deems necessary.

Guest Lists

These weddings have no guest lists. To the extent that anyone is invited, a couple of close friends or relatives can be asked to appear as witnesses. The moment couples start trying to expand this circle to include people beyond immediate family or the closest friends is the moment of their downfall. If no one is invited, no one can be sad about being left out of the inner circle.

Parties

It does look a bit odd to have an *engagement party* followed by an elopement, so the only reason to do this is if you are truly planning on having a traditional wedding and then discover, months down the line, that you simply can't. You risk people thinking you are strange, but if events conspired against you, that's all the explanation you need. On the other hand, if you are planning an elopement from the get-go, it would be safest to forgo the engagement party.

Bridal showers and elopements don't mix, because of the policy of inviting only people who will attend the wedding to the shower. So if you're planning to go to city hall, forget the shower. The exception to this policy is if you're having a postelopement reception. In that case, a bridal shower would be weird but not actively rude, as long as the shower guest list includes only people who are invited to the reception as well. If anyone expresses, through the gentle art of snark, some awkwardness about your decision, feel free to fall back on the tried-and-true reply that should be part of everyone's arsenal of nonwitty but effective retorts: "I'm sorry you feel that way. Would you like some cake?"

If it is good enough for traditionalists, it is certainly safe for contemporary elopers to have *receptions* to celebrate their marriages. These parties can take many forms. They can be completely informal bashes or formal wedding-type receptions. If the couple wants a big wedding cake, they can have it and eat it. If the new bride wants to wear a wedding dress, she can indulge her desires.

Presents

The big secret about wedding presents is that they are, as a general matter, optional (for much more on this subject, go to chapter 9, "Asking, Giving, and Getting: The Politics of Registries and Wedding Presents"). In the case of elopements, the question is not whether it is appropriate to send a present, but whether people want to. Of course, if there is a reception, there is a greater chance that guests will be moved to give wedding presents, but it is still no guarantee. For some the absence of a proper wedding, with a ceremony and all the trimmings, is a gift-giving deal breaker. It is never rude, however, to send a card indicating one's pleasure at the couple's union.

As with every other kind of wedding, it's crass for couples to be overly zealous about soliciting presents. In the case of elopements, the couple can set up registries and disperse this information through the proper grapevine channels (family and friends), but to aggressively solicit presents after eloping is unpleasant.

Destination Dynamics

Destination weddings differ from regular nuptials only in logistics. For the most part, all the rules of hometown weddings apply to those that take place abroad, except that there is very little room for dithering.

PLANNING

Destination weddings demand a lot of planning from everyone: bride, groom, guests, parents, officiants, employees at the actual venues. No one should minimize how much time is needed to structure a major event happening in a faraway place, even if the guest list is supposedly "intimate."

Hosts should let prospective guests know as soon as possible what plans are afoot. This is a case where save-the-date cards, indeed whole envelopes packed with information, should be sent out months in advance containing all kinds of details about when and where the wedding will take place, what airlines are the best carriers to get there, where one can stay (with luxurious and cheaper choices if possible), and some information about how to get around. Guests need to make flight and hotel reservations, but they also may need to negotiate vacation time and child care (if they're leaving the kids at home), renew long-expired passports, lose weight, gain weight, buy an appropriate wedding outfit . . . those sorts of things.

PARTIES

Unlike elopements, which operate on the fringe of nuptial convention, destination weddings can easily be accompanied by all the traditional events without anyone raising an eyebrow.

DON'T TAKE IT PERSONALLY

There's no question that it is easier for some people to hit the road than others. As a result, destination weddings can dredge up all kinds of strange feelings. These should all be put in perspective and, if possible, put aside.

If you are having a destination wedding and some people you truly love can't attend, do not hold it against them. Do not try to weigh their reasons for not going to your wedding against some sort of standard of behavior. Anything could be going on that you don't know about: financial troubles, work issues, child-care problems, health concerns . . . pique. If it is a case of your wedding versus their lives, the choice is pretty easy. Let it go.

If you've received an invitation to a wedding in sunny Italy and your heart has dropped into your stomach, don't take it personally if the trip is out of your means or logistically impossible for you. Your friends didn't decide to get hitched abroad because their secret Spidey sense told them it was inconvenient for you or because they wanted to test your affection for them. If it is too difficult for you to swing the trip, beg off. Don't be angry, just be gentle and honest and treat your marrying friends as if they are reasonable people who will understand your limitations. You don't have to come up with elaborate justifications. Wish them the best and indulge them by looking at their wedding pictures when they get back.

======   *Etiquette in Action*   ======

SHOULD WE JUST ELOPE?

Dear Elise,

My fiancé and I are trying to plan how we're going to get married. We are paying for everything ourselves and cannot afford a big, ornate wedding. Our families are both huge. We have seriously considered elopement. It sounds so peaceful, but will people feel left out? Help!

—Family Overload

Dear FO,

There is no shame in eloping, or having a courthouse wedding, especially when you're up against overwhelming family numbers.

There is a discreet middle ground you can consider, but you must be absolutely strict and rigid about it. You could have a parents-only wedding or immediate-family-only wedding, where you permit literally only either parents or parents and siblings (and their significant others).

As far as how to celebrate your marriage with your families, you could send out announcements after your wedding and arrange to have some easy, inexpensive get-togethers with various groups of relatives and friends. How you arrange things is really up to you, as long as you remember to treat both families (yours and your fiancé's) with complete evenhandedness. If you are open with your family about your limitations and your interest in alternative celebrations, you will have done everything you could to protect everyone's feelings and your bank accounts.

THE QUESTIONABLE WISDOM OF A POSTWEDDING SHOWER

Dear Elise,

I want to throw a shower for my daughter and her fiancé, who are engaged and will be eloping. I am considering combining a shower and a wedding reception. Is this inappropriate?

—Concerned Mom

Dear Concerned Mom,

Showers are tricky, because they are parties that require presents. This generally means that it is a bad idea to invite anyone to a shower who isn't on the wedding guest list as well. Showers are also held before weddings, so having one after the fact is a bit peculiar.

In the case of an elopement and reception, you're in slightly safer territory, because there will be no one at all on the wedding guest list. In order for you to throw a shower and reception, you would be best off splitting up the events and throwing the shower before the elopement, while making sure that everyone on your shower guest list is also on your postelopement reception guest list. You may still hear some grumbling, and you are leaving yourself open to gift-grabbing accusations (especially since you are the mother of the bride, and mothers are traditionally not supposed to host showers for their daughters), but you will hear less than if you were to throw a shower-reception after the wedding.

If you want to be absolutely safe, have a reception party *only* and indicate on the invitation that this is a postwedding reception. The guests who are moved to do so will bring wedding presents without feeling pressured, and you won't have done anything questionable or weird. It is much better to have a party with no strings attached and let people know what they'll be celebrating, and see what happens.

POSTELOPEMENT SARTORIAL OPTIONS

Dear Elise,

My fiancé and I are eloping and having a reception when we get home. What do I wear?

—Fashion Victim

Dear Fashion Victim,

You can wear whatever you like. Many people decide to give their wedding dresses a second outing. If that isn't to your taste, or if you didn't have a wedding dress, you could always let the party you're throwing be your guide to sartorial selections. Cocktail parties could inspire cocktail dresses; if you're having dinner and dancing and there's a gown you've had your eye on, go for it.

WORRIED ABOUT RELATIVES

Hi Elise,

My boyfriend and I have decided to get married at city hall, because this is the only way he can legally remain in the country. We plan on getting engaged (even though we'll already be married) within the next year or two, depending on finances; a wedding will follow.

I'm from a small town with a gossipy family. I don't want my extended family to be insulted about not being invited to our wedding, and we do want to have a huge shindig once we "really" get married. How do I explain that we really love each other, we will have a wedding and reception at some point, and our marriage isn't a sham—without looking like we're planning a future gift grab?

—Trying to Spare Everyone's Feelings

Dear Trying,

You're letting your family intimidate you. What you propose isn't wildly unusual. People elope for all sorts of reasons, some practical and some romantic, so don't think that your decision is anything less than legitimate.

Tell your relatives that this plan is what works best for you and that you will be thrilled to have them come to your big reception when you do have it. Keep these conversations simple and emphasize how happy you are with your plans. If you get defensive, people will wonder what secret unhappiness is making you so sensitive, and even if there is none, someone will make something up.

Do what feels best and what you need to do, be honest about your choices, and let the people whose feelings are most likely to be hurt know what you're planning ahead of time so they don't feel blindsided.

HOW TO ANNOUNCE WHEN THE WEDDING WAS A SECRET

Dear Elise,

My parents offered to finance a wedding for my now-husband and me after we announced our engagement. A few months after we got engaged, we were compelled to marry ahead of our schedule (for insurance, among other reasons).

We didn't want to hurt any feelings, so we decided to proceed with the "public" wedding as planned and keep our courthouse marriage secret.

Months later, my parents decided that they couldn't afford to host our wedding, and we, in turn, made our families aware of our marriage. All of our parents freaked out.

Our friends do not know that we have been secretly married. We would still like to plan something to include our loved ones in our marriage, but are not sure what to do and really can't afford to host a party right now. We were thinking of sending announcements around our anniversary this year to let people know we've married and are perhaps planning a vow renewal ceremony. Is this appropriate? Should we indicate on the announcements that we got married?

—Courthouse Bride

Dear Courthouse Bride,

There is nothing wrong with being married. That is the most important thing to remember in all of this. Your parents were no doubt put out by the fact that you got married secretly. There are surely some control issues at work, since only after they withdrew funding for your wedding did you tell them that you were already married, so they perhaps have the sense that you might have tried to put something over on them. At this point, they should grow up and be happy that you're happy and get over your few months of secrecy.

Now, wedding announcements are best sent immediately (or as soon as possible) after the wedding. For you to issue announcements out of the blue would seem odd. Odder still would be sending announcements that contain the suggestion that you may throw a party at some point in the future, but without any real plan. That will only confuse everyone. This is not a good idea.

Instead, take a casual approach. Let people know in conversation that you got married a while ago and then, when you are ready, throw a party celebrating your commitment, and you can certainly mention your wedding, or at least the fact that you're married, in your invitations.

Understand that you don't have to have a big, formal affair. There are plenty of reasonable, nontraditional options that will suit you well. And be sure to invite your parents to the festivities. Proving to them that you weren't waiting on their cash to celebrate your union is a significant gesture, and including them definitively says that you aren't embarrassed by your decisions. Which you shouldn't be.

COVERING DESTINATION EVENTS

Hello Elise,

What is the proper way to invite a few people (only special friends and family) to a Friday evening out-of-town wedding? Are the bride and groom obliged to pay for the evening before and after the wedding? Should some itinerary be planned for the guests for the entire weekend, since the event is taking place out of town?

—Making Plans

Dear MP,

What you have on your hands is a destination wedding, and there are many ways to approach this kind of event. Unless you are planning a structured weekend, with lots of invite-only events (rehearsal dinner, morning-after brunch, that sort of thing), you are only responsible for paying for the wedding and reception. You should pay for the events to which you invite everyone.

As a courtesy, you can give your guests a list of things they can do while they're in the area. If they decide to make a weekend of it, they can enjoy the local attractions, or they can just turn around and head home. That leaves questions of plans and entertainment up to your guests, and you will have been entirely gracious.

ELOPING AND THE REGISTRY

Dear Elise,

My fiancé and I just decided to elope. We are going to invite only two friends to be our witnesses. My problem is, we don't know when we should tell people about the elopement. I initially thought we would send out wedding announcements and invitations to a postelopement reception when we got back. But my fiancé says we should tell everyone now and have someone throw me a shower so we can register for presents.

If I were to tell everyone and have a shower, should I still do the wedding announcement and/or reception invitation postelopement?

—Hitting the Road

Dear Hitting the Road,

You are in an interesting position, but it isn't an unusual one. You're eloping, which means you aren't going to invite anyone to your wedding. You don't have to be secretive about it. However, eloping does affect the way you approach your announcement plans.

First of all, you shouldn't send out an announcement that you are eloping. After the fact, you can certainly mail a wedding announcement, and you can send it alone or with an invitation to your postelopement reception.

As far as showers and registering are concerned, you can absolutely register for presents, and people who come to your postelopement party will probably be inclined to give presents, but it would be rather problematic to count on a shower. Bridal showers, because of the gift requirements, are really meant to have a guest list of people who are invited to the wedding. In some elopement situations, you can have a shower, but only if you are organized enough to have your reception set up before you elope, so that your guests know they are not being soaked for presents in honor of an event that will ultimately be excluding them.

The best, most polite thing to do is to tell people casually about your plans simply because you're happy and excited and to wait for the rest until you are married. You'll spare yourselves all kinds of confusion.

Chapter 6

Guess Who's Coming:
Guest List Negotiations

Prepare for battle.

The wedding guest list is often the place where all interested parties—from brides to grooms to mothers to guests to the adult spokespeople for squalling infants—first cross swords. It makes sense that this would be the first sticking point. This is the moment when those involved start making up lists of friends and relatives and deciding how important each person really is. There is a lot of competition and comparison. Should the bigger family necessarily be entitled to more invitations? What if the groom has a lot more friends than the bride?

Even guests aren't immune to the numbers game. Will they be able to bring dates or children? What if they want to use their "plus one" to bring someone the bride and groom can't stand? Is it fair to ask someone to fly solo at a wedding? Does fairness matter when faced with grim numbers about how much the caterer charges per head? Each potential guest becomes not just a person, but also a negotiating point, and the bigger the guest list, the greater the potential for headaches.

Traditional Basics

- The wedding guest list is actually the compilation of four separate lists. The bride, the groom, the bride's family, and the groom's family each generates a dream list of invitees. From these a master list is born.
- Depending on how inclusive each part of the wedding is, the list gets broken into categories, including guests who will be invited to the wedding and the reception; guests who will only be invited to the large wedding ceremony (this applies primarily to close communities with a large central house of worship); guests who will not be invited to an intimate ceremony but who will be invited to the reception; and people who will receive no invitations but who will be sent a wedding announcement and the wedding couple's "at-home" card. (For more on nuptial-related stationery, see chapter 8, "In Print: Wedding Stationery and What to Write on It.")
- Standard candidates for guest lists are: relatives of the bride and groom, friends of both families, friends of the bride and groom, neighbors, and business associates.
- Even though they surely know they are invited, all members of the wedding party, the officiant (and his or her spouse), and the groom's parents receive invitations.
- The hosts (meaning the people who are paying for the wedding) determine the size of the event and are in charge of figuring out approximately how many people each of the interested parties can invite.
- After an initial wave of responses comes in (with, presumably, a few negatives), a second wave of invitations can be sent. All remaining invitations should be sent at least two and a half weeks before the wedding.
- Guests should not ask to bring dates unless the date is a substitute for

an invited spouse or relative, and they must ask their hosts ahead of time if the swap can be made.

Twisting Tradition

So those rules seem fair enough, as far as they go, but they don't begin to address all the intricacies of contemporary guest list negotiations. In the first place, it is hardly a given anymore to assume that the bride's family is footing the bill for the whole affair. Keep in mind that many wedding traditions are the product of populations that were relatively static. Now families not only break apart with unfortunate regularity, but even happy ones are spread all over the world, and weddings themselves often happen in far-flung locales. Traditional etiquette may live on, but the laws need an overhaul.

There is one element from the past that remains constant, and both hosts and guests should always keep it in mind: An invitation is a good thing. Just look at the standard language: "the honor of your presence" or "the pleasure of your company" is requested. How could that be an insult? Everyone should banish any negative thoughts about "gift grabs" or "status seeking" when it comes to guest lists. Some invitations will always be obligations, and some guests will always have to attend things out of duty, but an invitation should be considered a nice gesture. The opposite is also true. Wedding hosts are often forced to make all sorts of hard decisions and cut their guest lists down, sacrificing the company of people they care about and would love to have at their weddings for that of annoying relatives in order to preserve peace in the family.

Planning

The guest list really can only be determined by first deciding the size of the wedding, and the people who set these numbers are the ones who will be paying. It is really only fair to handle it this way. Of course there is room for negotiation, and if other parties want to contribute, then the guest list can be increased.

As the wrangling goes forward, it is important to keep in mind that the wedding is not a popularity contest. If there are huge discrepancies in the sizes of the bride's and the groom's families, that's fine. The sides don't have to be even. It is gracious for the smaller family to cut the larger family some slack and not be petty about numbers. (A wedding myth that has no basis in tradition is that the bride's family gets to determine the lion's share of the invites. This is not automatically the case. So don't allow anyone to trot out that "rule" as a way to secure more slots for their friends on the guest list.) Everyone wins if loved ones don't have to be excluded. If any guest actually wastes time counting sides, it is a sign that he or she isn't drinking, eating, or dancing enough.

Musts

There are few absolutes when it comes to wedding invitations. Couples don't even have to invite their parents if they don't want to. As a general matter, couples who are married or in committed relationships must be invited to weddings together. They are a unit and should be treated as such. We all have friends who have incredibly annoying spouses, but the unpleasant partners still have to be included on guest lists if you want to include your friends. Happily, the nuptial bustle at the reception goes a long way toward minimizing the amount of time you must spend with the irritating and obnoxious companions of people you actually like. There are just too many people to deal with for you to have sustained contact with anyone disagreeable.

In addition, guests should keep in mind that their dates are not interchangeable, as traditional etiquette insists. If your partner is not available, you must ask your hosts if someone else can come on your arm.

Kid Limits

Children are divisive. They don't mean to be, and it isn't their fault, but they've become a "love 'em or hate 'em" wedding element, and if you hate them, you need to find a way to draw the line.

If you want a completely child-free wedding, the first step is to make the event unappealing to kids and encourage the parents to find sitters. Evening weddings where the festivities roll late into the night are difficult for children. Who wants to have to let a drowsy toddler pass out on a pile of coats somewhere or split early because the kid's missed bedtime has turned the tiny charmer into the Antichrist? A late hour is an innocent, nonconfrontational signal for guests to find babysitters.

As far as invitations go, it is never a good idea to print "No kids allowed" on your cards. There's no gentle way to say it, and you'll only come off as somewhat hostile. When you address your invitations, include only the names of the parents on the envelopes. If you're concerned your guests won't get the hint, you should give the parents a call or include a brief, handwritten, personal note indicating that you can't accommodate children at the wedding. If your friends return their response cards indicating that they intend to bring their kids, then you must take action. Call them and explain your policy. Make it clear that you don't have a problem with their kids, but you simply are stuck in an "everyone or no one" situation and have been forced to exclude all children for the sake of a peaceful kingdom.

Just because there are ways to exclude kids doesn't mean there won't be any fallout. Some parents will find a way to be insulted that their children weren't included in your nuptials. They may boycott or threaten to boycott. You must stand firm. If you stray from your policy at all, the kid floodgates will burst open and you'll have to invite all of them. On the other hand, some people will not be able to attend if their children can't, and you must accept that possibility. If travel is involved, it may be impossible for parents to find child care. You may lose a few guests as a result of your choice, but if you're sympathetic and gentle, you won't lose friends.

What if you want some kids around but not others? Do you feel the ice starting to crack under your feet? Really, there are a couple of ways to do this, but there is one unbreakable rule: *You must be absolutely, rigidly consistent and make no exceptions.* If you make exceptions, you are doomed to Never Hearing the End of It.

One way to ensure that only a few children will attend is to invite only the offspring of immediate family: your own kids, your nephews and nieces, your half siblings (if there are any), and that's it. Alternatively, you could draw the line at the children of immediate family and the kids of wedding party members. Another choice that is much dodgier is to have an age cutoff. To do this, you have to really carefully consider your guest pool, because if there are a lot of sibling sets where the younger child will have to stay home, this policy can generate all kinds of strife. Because it can get you into more hot water than simply excluding all children, use this last option only if you are sure you won't get a lot of flak for creating not only the need for a babysitter, but also a potential sibling rivalry issue.

Office Invitations

It isn't hard to feel conflicted about whether or not to invite coworkers to a wedding. Mingling one's public and private spheres can be uncomfortable.

Even though you've talked about your wedding plans with your colleagues for months, just imagine returning to work after your boss has committed all the toasts to memory—including the one where your best friend trotted out some horror story about your short-lived love affair with black Sambuca in high school.

If this inspires more fear than enthusiasm, you should know that you can choose not to invite your coworkers to your wedding. As with children, the easiest and most inoffensive route to adopt is an "everyone or no one" policy. This way, no one can feel left out and insulted, which can create future office awkwardness. (Clearly, asking "everyone" means different things in different work environments. You could find yourself inviting an entire office if the company is small, or just your immediate team and supervisors if you're in a larger corporate setting.)

Should you decide to invite just a few colleagues, you absolutely must be discreet. Remember that mortifying moment in grammar school when you were the only one not invited to some fancy birthday party? This is not a time to reenact that drama by casting yourself as the popular party giver. All of your correspondence (save-the-date cards, invitations, etc.) must go in the mail. Do not leave them on desks, and do not make your wedding Topic A at lunch. In addition, you should tell the few people you are inviting that you are excluding the bulk of the office and beg them not to mention your wedding to other people. It can be risky if some of the people you're inviting are blabbermouths, flaky, or inclined to be socially savage, but at least you will know that you have done everything possible to protect your colleagues' feelings. While it is not necessary to invite your coworkers to your wedding, if you decide to go that route, it is polite to invite your boss or your immediate supervisor as well.

And Guest?

As a general matter, the way to understand who is invited to a wedding is to look at the envelope the invitation arrived in. The people to whom it is addressed are the people whose presence is requested. No one else should be added or swapped out. You shouldn't bring children, friends visiting from abroad, or distant relatives who feel slighted. Nor should you exchange one boyfriend for another or a wife for a girlfriend without talking to the wedding couple or your hosts and getting their approval. It is, after all, their party.

Traditional etiquette frowns on wedding invitations that go out addressed to someone "and Guest." The reasoning behind the furrowed brow is that everyone invited should be known, if only by name, either to the wedding hosts or the wedding couple.

That attitude is optimistic, however, and if you are in a position to invite single friends and relatives to bring dates, you can write "and Guest" on their invitation envelopes. If you can't afford to budget for a mystery date for every single guest, you don't need to offer this courtesy. The choice depends entirely on your abilities, though as in all things nuptial, you must be consistent. All single people should have the same courtesy, because if it gets around that you're playing favorites somehow, you'll Never Hear the End of It.

You should not write "and Guest" on invitations to people who already have significant others just because you are too lazy to find out what those people's last names are. You still have to make those calls.

If you're on the receiving end of an "and Guest" invitation, you are free to attend the wedding with anyone you like on your arm, but when you reply to the invitation, you should reveal your date's name. Your hosts will need it if they make a seating plan for the reception.

Presumptuous People

"Oh! You're getting married in June! Well, you better tell me exactly what date, because we're going to Paris next summer and I wouldn't want to miss your wedding." Imagine these words popping out of the mouth of someone you have absolutely no intention of inviting to your wedding (or possibly anything else). Are you stuck? What do you say? You have to learn the Language of Weddings. It is a gentle code, easy to master and understand.

When faced with an aggressive invitation pursuer, say only, "We're having a very small wedding" or "It is very hard to settle on a guest list that satisfies all the families." Then change the subject completely and do not elaborate any further on your wedding plans. Make no further excuses. Don't stop being perfectly pleasant, but from that moment on, all wedding talk with the presumptuous friend must stop.

The Infernal Add-On

So often, people are told to reject the word "No," to close their ears to the possibility that what they want is either impossible or simply not going to happen. This strategy is an enormous drag when it comes to wedding guests trying to co-opt the reception for their own private interests. They will try to do this in various ways. They will ask if they can bring some extra people. They will promise these extra people will forgo dinner (because they will assume the only objection you could have to these additional guests is financial). If they're afraid to ask you directly, they will return their invitation's response card with a list of extra names or merely "+6" written on it, hoping you won't notice the extra hordes.

You aren't required to accommodate additional guests. If you don't want them, stand your ground firmly. All you need to say is, "I'm sorry. We already have our guest list all planned and we can't accommodate anyone else." Do not apologize or explain any further. Doing that will only dig you into a hideous trench where you will be accused of being cheap, or someone clever will think he or she can have his or her way by sending you a check to cover all the people you didn't want to see in the first place. (And if you think that doesn't happen, you're sorely mistaken.)

Is It in the Mail?

You *thought* you were invited. The bride *told you* she was going to invite you. But the wedding is approaching, and your mailbox is stuffed with only catalogues and credit card offers. What should you do besides sit and think unpleasant things about your friend?

Generally, the mail is reliable, but anything can happen, so approach the problem with two goals in mind. First, give everyone the benefit of the doubt. It *is* possible that your invitation got rerouted, but it is also possible that your friends were forced to trim their guest list and you were an unfortunate casualty. You can absolutely contact them to find out what the score is. If they did have to cut you, they are surely feeling awful and embarrassed and won't know how to talk about it, but getting in touch will give them an opportunity to come clean, especially if you try to be understanding.

Once you've established whether or not you've made the cut, your second goal in this mess is to preserve your relationship (assuming you want to). There is no reason your friendship shouldn't continue, even if you didn't make the final guest list. The silver lining is that you have a free evening (or weekend), you don't have to come up with a present, and your friends will always be grateful that you were so graceful about their dopey behavior.

Balancing Acts and Cutoffs

Some interested party is always going to push for more invitations. Even if a wedding's size was determined shortly after the engagement, by the time invitations get ordered, people often forget what they were thinking in more temperate times. Sometimes the wedding couple wants to embrace the world. Other times, one or both sets of parents feels that it can't survive socially if it doesn't ask every neighbor, business connection, and distant relative to a child's wedding.

Something has to give, and usually that thing is the budget. At this point, etiquette must become practical. One can't invite people one can't afford to host, and one can't invite people who won't fit into the ceremony and reception venues.

Collaboration and compromise are necessary. Can the venue hold more people? Can the people who want to add twenty names offer to pay for them? It is much better to think of this question in practical terms rather than dig in your heels and say, "I only wanted seventy-six people at my wedding, and that's the way it is going to be!" If you can negotiate, try to find a way to include a few more people. Bending even a little bit goes a long way.

On the other hand, if you find that you are seriously limited and have 150 additional people you'd like to include but can't pack into your son's fiancée's family's backyard, consider having a private postwedding reception where you can call all the shots and set the guest list of your dreams. You can throw this bash any time after the wedding.

====================   *Etiquette in Action*   ====================

BROTHER DICTATES GUEST LIST?

Dear Elise,

My fiancé and I are trying to keep our wedding small, but my brother says we have to invite his wife's parents to our wedding because that's the way it is done within their social circles. We would rather not invite them.

We also decided to have a child-free wedding. My brother and sister-in-law have a son and have been saying how cute he'll look in a tux walking down the aisle! My sister-in-law's parents would babysit for my nephew over the wedding weekend, and if they came to our wedding, my brother would have no child care.

—Frustrated

Dear Frustrated,

You have to stand up to your brother. He already had a wedding. Now it is your turn, and it really doesn't matter what happens in his social circles.

It is not necessary to invite your sister-in-law's parents to your wedding. As long as you and your fiancé aren't planning on inviting the parents of other sibling-in-laws, you can't even be accused of showing any favoritism. Tell your brother in a reasonable amount of time that you won't be able to accommodate his extended family.

As for the question of your nephew, tell your brother sooner rather than later that you are not going to have children at your wedding. This issue is separate from the exclusion of his in-laws. Do not mention anything about his in-laws and babysitting. Who he gets to babysit his child is your brother's business. What you really must do is stick to your guns and not let your brother bully you. He doesn't have access to any special protocols that you don't know about.

THE TEARS OF DIVORCED GUESTS

Dear Elise,

Growing up, I had a good friend, and our families were very close. My parents are friendly with both of my friend's parents, even though they divorced.

My mother insisted that I invite both of my friend's parents. My friend could not come, but both of her parents said yes.

When my friend's mother found out that her ex-husband is planning to attend the wedding, she told my mother that she cannot be in the same room with him and is furious that no one told her that we invited both of them. My mother told her that she never wanted to hurt her but didn't want to have to choose between two friends, but this woman is still very upset. What should I do? I don't think I can "un-invite" anyone.

—Panicked

Dear Panicked,

You haven't done anything wrong or damaging. This friend's pain is making her act like a spoiled child, complete with tears and threats.

It is true that you or your mother would have been wise to warn your friend's mother that you were inviting her ex-husband to the wedding. That would have given her a chance to make an informed decision about whether or not she would attend. That is a small mistake, but this woman has no right to dictate the guest list for your wedding, and she is presumptuous in thinking that you and your parents are insulting her friendship. All you are doing is refusing to choose sides, and that is more than reasonable.

Reassure her that you care deeply about her and want her to attend your wedding. You can describe the steps you will take to ensure that she will not have to come into contact with her ex-husband (assigned seating at the reception, flanking her with people she knows and likes during the ceremony, etc.). If she says she simply can't bear to attend, tell her how deeply sorry you are, reiterate that you never meant to hurt her, and be as supportive as you can be.

Understand that you didn't do anything wicked. Divorced couples are often invited to the same events and manage to enjoy themselves without rekindling ire. It is not your responsibility to have to choose between them.

AVOIDING "AND GUEST"

Dear Elise,

My fiancé and I are planning on having a very small wedding ceremony, with a reception several months later. We would like to limit the reception guest list to about one hundred people.

Do we have to let all single people bring dates? I do not want a lot of people I don't know attending. I will be inviting friends' and relatives' significant others whom I have met and with whom I am also friendly, so it seems unfair to allow these people dates and not others. I have heard that it's okay to address wedding invites to specific people. But is it really okay to address invites to singles without adding on "and Guest"?

Thanks,

—Keeping Numbers Down

Dear KND,

The key to solving the "and Guest" question is in setting a policy, though the "I only want to invite people I know and like" route is not the right approach to take.

Traditional etiquette holds that one should address all invitations by name. This means that you wouldn't use the "and Guest" construction, but you would have to ask your guests for the correct spelling of their partners' names. This is easy for guests who are married or who are in committed relationships with people you know (and like). With your unattached friends, you don't have to allow them to bring dates, but you must be consistent. If you allow some people who are not in firmly established relationships to bring dates, you should extend that courtesy to everyone. (People try to make arbitrary rules, such as creating age cutoffs for teenagers' dates, but fundamentally, once you are inviting adults to your wedding you must decide whether all of the single grown-ups can bring dates or not.) You must draw clear lines so people don't feel that you are playing favorites.

THE UNINVITED

Dear Elise,

My fiancée and I are planning a tiny wedding. We want only our closest friends around us, and our guest list does *not* include a friend of mine whose interests run primarily toward drinking and random hookups. I think if I don't invite this person, a mutual friend will either invite our acquaintance or bring her as a "surprise." How can I make it clear to our mutual friend that I won't be inviting this person and would prefer if she weren't in attendance?

—Between a Rock and a Hard Place

Dear Between,

Does this friend—the person you actually want to invite—really strike you as the kind of person who would just start inviting people to crash your wedding? If there is any history of that kind of stunt, there's no reason not to be proactive.

Tell your friend that your guest list is extremely restricted, and explain that you can't include anyone else because doing so would trigger all sorts of anger and jealousy in relatives and friends, all of whom will feel snubbed and left out if the guest list is expanded even a little bit. Lay it on thick. You can say that you are asking all of your guests to be discreet about your plans and emphasize how important it is to you that the guest list not be mucked with or added to by anyone for any reason. Understand, however, that if you are allowing your single guests to bring dates, you really can't dictate who they decide to choose as their escorts. In a situation like yours, where you suspect someone will be invited as a practical joke, you can ask your friend to respect your feelings.

FRIENDS IN THREESOMES

Hi Elise,

I have two sets of friends who live in threesomes. I don't know how to invite them to my wedding. In one case, a friend is involved with a married couple. In the other, a married couple with whom I am friendly added a third person.

I don't think their choices are immoral, but it will be tricky explaining so many extra guests to my family. I also don't want to have people I don't like or hardly know come to my wedding since I'm also trying to keep the guest list short.

—Too Many Plus Ones

Dear Too Many,

The traditional line—which is a decent starting point, even in cases that seem to be antitraditional—is that friends should be invited with their spouses or the partners with whom they are in committed relationships. Usually, living with someone constitutes a committed relationship. It really is bad news to exclude half of a married couple, even if one doesn't care for the person.

In the case of your friends, however, you have these communal romances to negotiate, and your choices depend on your knowledge of your friends. If you are feeling inclusive but holding back primarily because of your family's reaction, consider that there are really only three extra guests (your friend's married couple and your married friends' extra person). You could conceivably slip them under your family's noses.

How established are these trios? Do they expect to be invited to events together or is their situation a private arrangement that they keep at home? If you are not inviting single people to come with "guests," you have a better chance of just being able to invite your single friend and your married friends without their extras, but really, it all depends on how these groups exist in their relationships, what sorts of commitments they've made to one another, and how public they are about those commitments.

You'll do best if you clear your mind of distracting protests. It is very hard to have a wedding where at least a few faces are not ultrafamiliar, and it is even harder to have a wedding where one is fond of everyone's significant other or others.

You know your friends and seem aware of their sensitivities, and this is a case where you will be best guided by instinct and conversation. Inviting everyone is the safest and most generous route to take (and the whole lot might not come anyway), but only you and they know the states of these relationships, how committed they are, how public they are, and how they would react to an invitation that is either inclusive or restrictive.

Chapter 7

Brass Tacks: Planning Principles

It is hard to overcome the forces of tradition, particularly when they're commanding you to spend all kinds of money in the name of having a "perfect" wedding or being the "perfect" guest. The Wedding-Industrial Complex has worked very hard to generate needs where there are none and preys on the insecurity everyone harbors about the unfamiliar.

So. Where does one start planning a wedding? All it takes are a few brief moments of consideration to realize the whole business is a house of cards—each piece depends on the others in order to stand up and make the rest of the plans possible. Family, bridal party members, and friends are also left with obligations when faced with an upcoming wedding, so don't assume you have nothing to think about just because you're not the one getting hitched.

Two things should help you keep everything in perspective. First, to get *married*, all you truly need is a valid marriage license, someone who is legally capable of performing the ceremony, and (if necessary) witnesses. And second, to have a *wedding*, you need to strategize, or find someone to do it for you.

Traditional Basics

There are two elements that are easy to overlook in traditional etiquette books, and these facts can wind up producing a lot of confusion for contemporary people if they're not recognized and if the advice is not taken with the requisite grain of salt. Most old-fashioned etiquette assumes (1) that people are getting married in a church or a church-type locale, and (2) that people are getting married close to where the bride's and groom's families live. So if you're feeling classical and rigid, but still have to leave town, beware and be aware—the following traditional protocol might not work for you. Traditional etiquette says:

- The families of both bride and groom should be pleased with the proceedings, but the bride and groom should have the final word (assuming that their requirements don't tax their hosts beyond their means or profoundly offend their beliefs).
- Assuming the bride's family is paying for the event, the groom's family can offer to contribute to the wedding budget, but the bride's family should not ask for money.
- The two biggest initial points of negotiation tend to be how large and how formal the wedding will be.
- It is easiest to start planning by picking the season and the location of the ceremony (whether it be in a house of worship, city hall, an outdoor space, or some venue that will also host the reception).
- Standard questions to think about regarding the ceremony and ceremony venue are: Who will perform the ceremony? What kind of ceremony will it be? How long will the ceremony be? How many guests can the ceremony venue hold (and seat) comfortably? How will the guests get from the

ceremony to the reception? How long a time interval between ceremony and reception is comfortable?

- Standard questions to think about regarding the reception venue are: How many people will you host? What type of food will you serve? Will you be able to serve alcoholic drinks if you want to? What is the deadline for a guest head count? Will there be dancing? Is there space for a band or DJ?

- If a reception is held at a standard mealtime, then a meal must be served. (See chapter 14, "Sustenance and Civility: The Ins and Outs of the Wedding Reception" for explicit information about receptions and food.)

- Guests who come to town for the wedding are obliged to pay for their own transportation and accommodations. The wedding hosts can help by arranging for local friends or relatives to put up the out-of-towners, but this gesture is not required and not always possible.

Twisting Tradition

The traditional protocols regarding wedding planning are both vague and scarce. At the heart of most contemporary wedding planning are questions about money and how much one should equate money with control. It is very easy to use finances as a weapon and threaten to withhold cash if plans aren't going precisely your way, but no matter who is controlling the purse strings, it would be wise to relax, be a bit flexible, and refrain from burning bridges out of pique. There is plenty of room for unconventional weddings, and the only obstacle to them is whether or not friends and family can get into the spirit of celebrating with a little novelty instead of being obnoxious or sullen about it.

When? Where?

There is no perfect time to get married. No matter what you plan, someone is going to be inconvenienced or unable to attend. Everyone must accept this, so don't be offended if people can't come to your wedding. If you're a prospective guest, don't be angry at people who decide to get married in another country when you're broke or who annoyingly arrange their nuptials while you'll be at your grandparents' fiftieth wedding anniversary eleven states away. This will happen.

If you are planning a wedding, try not to ask many people if they will be available for your nuptials. It seems like a great courtesy, but what you will actually be doing is making yourself vulnerable to other peoples' whims and schedules. If you inquire, your prospective guests will certainly tell you about their exam schedules, vacation plans, hopes to be too pregnant to fly . . . and then you'll either feel obliged to work around these people you love, or you'll be angry that they can't just make themselves available. There are exceptions, of course. If there are people without whom you can't imagine your wedding, you should absolutely consult with them, but keep the circle of people who have a stake in your decisions small, or risk seeing them sulk when you go your own way.

If you have not been consulted and find that your friends or relatives have planned a wedding you can't attend, be honest but not petulant about your disappointment. Tell the truth about how torn you are about your conflicting plans or your inability to travel, but do not expect things to change. The wedding couple may have too many compelling reasons for getting married in Belize over Labor Day weekend to change their minds, and they aren't getting married for your convenience anyway.

Officiant Selection

As you start to plan your wedding, something you should deal with sooner rather than later is what sort of ceremony you will have and, by extension, who will have the honor of conducting it. This is not necessarily the easiest issue to resolve, since it can involve the spiritual beliefs of any number of wedding contributors, so it's wise to wrestle with this question early. Do you both want a religious ceremony? Do you both prefer secular proceedings? Do you both participate in the same religion? If you don't, is it important to both of you that your individual religious beliefs are reflected in the ceremony? What do you care most about? What aspects of your religion's ceremony are most significant to you? Do you hope to have a dual ceremony that addresses both your faiths, or two completely separate ceremonies? Will your beliefs permit a ceremony that combines with that of another faith? Hash it out.

Occasionally a rigorous absence of belief can be more difficult to deal with than two separate religions. If one part of a couple feels strongly about having a religious ceremony (and this can happen for a host of reasons: actual belief, family influence and obligation, a desire to participate in a tradition, an interest in doing what is most comfortable) and the other part of the couple is aggressively antireligion, a resolution must be unearthed. The key will be to negotiate with the atheist about how to handle these conflicting desires. There could be two ceremonies: one secular and one that participates in the religion, or there could be a dual ceremony (this would obviously not work if the religion in question requires that someone convert or express faith).

For many, the ceremony is a huge area of compromise, and unfortunately religion often makes people reluctant or unable to negotiate. Everyone—bride, groom, parents, relatives—should try to make small accommodations in the name of peace, for the sake of the wedding couple, and with an eye toward a nondivisive future.

Who Goes First?

Weddings can be contagious within social sets and families, and it should come as no surprise if your friends and even siblings get engaged around the same time you do. This inevitably generates useless competition. Who gets married first? Does anyone get "dibs" on one date or another?

This is really a "first come, first served" situation. There is no other way to go about it fairly. Unless you are from a culture or family that insists that children marry in order of oldest to youngest, or are from a group of friends where you have some kind of blood pact about who must get married first, the people who make up their minds first and reserve their venues first are entitled to make plans without having to get "permission" from everyone else. This can be a bit tough to swallow for people who have been engaged longer or are just indecisive, but it is the only reasonable way to go about things.

Keep in mind that there is no competition to get married in a rush or in a specific order. No one needs to race to the altar or build up resentment that someone "stole" the date you were contemplating. These things happen, and it isn't the end of the world. If there are two weddings in one summer and relatives can travel only once, then some decisions need to be made about whether to have both events on the same weekend in the same general vicinity, so that everyone can attend. For anyone starting to peep about weddings on consecutive days, remember: You get one day in which to get married. The world continues to turn, and other people are entitled to make plans around your day. If close temporal and/or geographical proximity of weddings bothers you, you could always push your wedding date further into the future. No one should attempt to bully someone out of a date that has been chosen and booked. Every plan comes with trade-offs and compromises, and guest availability is just one of those elements one must contemplate.

Copycats

"She's copying me!" is a familiar cry among second graders, but one hears it occasionally when brides share, or over-share, their wedding plans. Sometimes the copying is aggressive, competitive, and creepy in an *All About Eve* sort of way, and other times it can just be the result of someone needing an idea and seizing upon the first good one to come her or his way.

There is no question that copycats can be annoying. The only solution is to nip it in the bud. Stop discussing plans. If pressed, explain that you really want your wedding to be surprising and original and that you just aren't talking about it anymore. Imitation and flattery go hand in hand when it comes to nuptial self-expression. Weddings make people insecure, and to know that someone else has embraced a style makes it safe and comfortable. If you really want all of your choices to be utterly unique to your wedding, keep your mouth shut.

Themes

Your wedding doesn't need a theme, and anyone who tells you that it does should be sent back to that special hell that is high school and have to relive negotiating the senior prom theme every day for a month. Of course, if you *want* a themed wedding, don't be deterred—just brace yourself for the extra work.

Reception Variations

The general assumption is that wedding receptions happen at mealtimes, so people, not entirely unreasonably, tend to think they'll be tucking into a few courses. Depending on the size and style of the wedding, so many dedicated diners can be expensive, and it may be worth entertaining a few alternatives.

What many people don't realize is that a wedding followed by a serious meal is not a convention that needs to be maintained. As long as you warn your guests what they can expect in terms of sustenance, and plan your affair to avoid people becoming famished and cranky, you have many choices. You can have a teatime reception and offer light snacks and cake or cocktails and hors d'oeuvres, or skip everything and serve only dessert. For any of these mildly unusual receptions, your invitations should clue your guests in as to what they're signing up for. (For more on receptions, see chapter 14, "Sustenance and Civility: The Ins and Outs of the Wedding Reception.") You can easily indicate your alternative plans on invitations with small modifications to the standard reception invitation language.

Just a few words on the invitation will illuminate the style of reception guests can expect and can offset any possible laments they may harbor about the absence of the usual steak or chicken options. Include these details with the practical information about where and what time the reception will be held. Here are some examples:

- Please join us for cocktails and hors d'oeuvres at the Champagne Lounge at half past five
- Tea will be served in the garden following the ceremony
- A champagne toast and dessert will be served after the ceremony
- Join the wedding couple and their families for a late breakfast reception at eleven o'clock at the Mystery Kitchenette restaurant, 1165 Main Drive

Wedding Planners

Event planners are not necessary for all weddings, and you will likely know if you need one. If you are having a huge affair, need to do a lot of long-distance planning, don't have any time, don't want to make decisions alone, or are, for any other reason, utterly overwhelmed, entertain the thought of bringing in a professional. This is no defeat. You are hiring someone whose job is to be better at this than you are.

However, if you hire a wedding planner, you still have to do some work. You will need to develop a good idea of what you want your day to include and let your planner help you with the execution. Try to be open-minded while listening to reasonable suggestions. This is still your wedding, but some additional input and practical suggestions should not pose any threat to your vision. A planner should make sure you have the event you want—and won't let you forget your marriage license.

Gay Weddings

As far as etiquette goes, the issues that come up for gay weddings are largely the same as the problems that heterosexual nuptials face, with the exception of the obstacle of homophobia. In the United States there are still huge, often insurmountable, legal hurdles, so many gay weddings are, by necessity, destination affairs in other countries. In terms of protocol, however, there is no reason why people's basic manners should be any different for homosexual weddings than they are for heterosexual ones.

Etiquette in Action

RELIGIOUS DIFFERENCES

Hello Elise,

I am an atheist. My boyfriend is Muslim. We are planning on getting married, but I'm worried about how to handle our huge religious and cultural differences.

Most of the wedding guests will be from my family. Do I let my big family influence the wedding, do I give a nod to his religion and culture, or do I scrap it all and go with something totally different?

—Clash of Worlds

Dear Clash,

You face a sobering question: How much do you have to do to take care of your partner's feelings and accommodate his religion and culture? Have you talked to your fiancé about his preferences? This is certainly where you should begin.

Take the opportunity to have a larger conversation about the roles his Muslim beliefs and your atheism will play out in your lives together. If you have children, does he want them to be raised Muslim? Does he want them to know his cultural traditions but he doesn't care as much about the religious aspects? Does he not care at all? What do you want, and what are you willing to do?

Once you know your fiancé's inclinations, work on finding a middle ground where his religion and culture can be respected without requiring you to actively compromise your atheism. Once you've sorted that out, you can allow your family in, but letting them run roughshod over your wedding without figuring out where you and your fiancé need to set limits would be unwise.

In all likelihood, you and your fiancé will have to compromise a lot for your wedding. This is actually a good thing, since it will show you how to work with each other on small problems that reflect much deeper questions (like religious beliefs and family loyalty). Be patient with each other, and if something is nonnegotiable for you, see if there is another element you can compromise on for your future husband. Sometimes that is easier than changing people's minds—and more rewarding.

MYSTERY FATHER

Elise,

My partner and I just recently got engaged. My father always got along well with my girlfriend, but ever since I told him we were getting married, he has refused to talk about the wedding. I asked him if he wanted to contribute some money, but now I wonder if it was wrong. Is it weird that I expected him to be enthusiastic? I'm his only daughter.

Why would he change his mind about her so completely?

—A Confused Bride

Dear Confused Bride,

There is no telling what your father's problem may be.

He could be uncomfortable about the fact that you're marrying another woman to the point where his confusion is making him forget that he actually really likes your girlfriend. In another scenario, he may be upset that you are marrying anyone at all. Perhaps your engagement signifies beyond a doubt that you are grown up, which means that he must be "old," which depresses him. Anything could be making him act strangely.

You can quiz your father about his attitude, but if you approach him, brace yourself for answers that might not please you. Alternatively, you could give him some time to let him get used to the idea of your marriage, and maybe he'll settle back into his normal state without prodding.

The money is a completely separate issue. From where you sit, his feelings and his financial contributions seem to have a lot to do with each other, but try to think of them as unconnected issues. You didn't do anything wrong in asking your father if he wants to contribute to your wedding, but he is within his rights to tell you that he can't or won't be giving you any money. The best protection against his refusal is to tell yourself that you don't need his help. This may mean that you need to do a lot of contingency planning, but if he withholds cash, you will resent him less if you don't have to make big sacrifices.

Try to be patient with your father. Don't push too hard for his approval or his financial support. This may be one of those situations where the more independent you are, the more he will be inclined to step in and the less conflicted you will be about accepting him on whatever terms he offers.

HIS WANTS VERSUS MY WANTS

Dear Elise,

My fiancé and I don't see eye to eye about our upcoming wedding. I want something small, nontraditional, and secular, and I want to invite close family and friends and keep the event personal and fun.

My fiancé wants a ceremony in a church with a priest, because that's his idea of what a real wedding is. I would understand this if he were religious, but he isn't. I am agnostic, and I don't want a religious ceremony. How can I convince him to think about what *he* wants, without making him think I just don't like his ideas?

—Conundrum

Dear Conundrum,

You probably already know that your problem is not so much one of etiquette as it is of taste. This does not mean, however, that etiquette can't help you.

Weddings come in endless variety. There is nothing that "everyone" does, and the only things you are "supposed" to do are secure a marriage license ahead of time, find a legal officiant, and have some witnesses sign the form.

You and your fiancé will have to compromise, and to do that with some measure of satisfaction, you should each figure out what is, for each of you, the most important element of the wedding. Perhaps your fiancé feels that having a big guest list including everyone he feels he owes an invitation is crucial. Maybe you feel that having a religion-free ceremony is the only thing you deeply care about. Once you each know where the other stands, you can begin to negotiate.

Chapter 8

In Print: Wedding Stationery and What to Write on It

Stationers go into paroxysms of joy when wedding couples approach. The list of required—or so-called required—paper items is elaborate, daunting, and enormous. Many items are the stuff of ancient tradition (indeed, some flourishes, such as those little pieces of tissue paper that float over printed invitations, had practical purposes in an earlier century but are purely aesthetic gestures today). Other contemporary "musts" would seriously surprise the older generation that those things could ever be necessary.

Write-in informal invitations, save-the-date cards, wedding invitations, enclosure cards, ceremony programs, wedding announcements, thank-you cards, and "at-home" cards—does one *need* all of these things? And do technological substitutes—electronic invitations, wedding websites, and the like—clear up the tangles of information and etiquette or snarl them further?

Traditional Basics

Traditional wedding stationery is beyond rigorous. The language is strictly codified; terms of address are inflexible. The starched style may feel uncomfortable, but consider the hidden advantages: For one, all your guests will know what to expect and won't be confused. Here is how it all plays out.

Pre-Wedding-Event Invitations

- Invitations to early events (engagement parties, showers, etc.) are usually on commercial fill-in-the-blank cards. Rehearsal dinner invitations can be printed or simply customized on store-bought fill-in invitations. These do not get sent out until the wedding date approaches, certainly not until after the wedding invitations themselves have been sent (except for engagement party invites).

Save-the-Date Cards

- There is no traditional protocol for save-the-date cards, since the practice of sending them is relatively new.

- The language can be creative and free-form, but fundamentally should be clear about the important information: the *names* of the people getting married, the *date* people need to save, and the *location* of the future wedding. Excessive mystery and whimsy renders the card useless.

- Mail save-the-date cards to your guest list, and remember that this is, in effect, an invitation. People will be offended if they receive a save-the-date card and then are not invited to the wedding.

Wedding Invitations

- Wedding invitations are written in the third person and are sent "from" the wedding's hosts (traditionally, this means the bride's parents, but anyone who hosts can be listed).

- All words are written out in full, without abbreviations (use the full words: "Street" or "Avenue" or "Doctor" and do not use middle initials—use either people's full middle names or skip the initial entirely.

- Spell out numbers unless they are long. While one would write "the eighth of November," a long address could appear in numerals: "2674 Drury Lane." If you're including the year, write it out. Write out the time of day, using "half after" or "half past" (not "thirty") to refer to events that happen on the half hour.

- It is traditional but not necessary to use the British spelling for words like "honour" and "favour."

- When inviting guests to the wedding ceremony, one requests "the honour of your presence." When inviting guests to the reception, one asks for "the pleasure of your company."

- It is equally correct to write: "R.S.V.P.," "R.s.v.p.," "RSVP," or "The favour of a reply is requested."

- Invitations are generally printed on white, ivory, or cream-colored heavy-weight paper. The tissue-paper overlay that is still used occasionally is a hold-over from times when ink was more likely to blot. It is no longer necessary.

- Invitations traditionally are sent in two envelopes. The actual invitation and any other materials are inserted in an envelope, which is then placed in a slightly larger envelope that gets stamped and mailed. (This tradition, however, weakened as early as the mid-1940s in the United States because of wartime paper shortages, so even ultratraditionalists would not blink if only one envelope were used.) Names and addresses are handwritten.

- The *outer envelope* is addressed to the person or people one intends to invite. If a married or committed couple shares a last name, the invitation is addressed to "Mr. and Mrs. Thomas Henry." If they are married and have different surnames, the woman's name appears first. Their names appear on the same line. If the couple is unmarried, their names appear on separate lines (the woman's name above the man's). Children over thirteen who are invited typically receive their own invitations, but their names can also be included under their parents' names. If the family has several children and all of them are invited, they can also be invited with their own separate invitation. This envelope would be addressed to "The Misses" or "The Messrs." If there are boys and girls to be invited the envelope is addressed to:

> *The Messrs. Rackstraw*
>
> *The Misses Rackstraw*

An envelope addressed to a married couple "and Family" implies that the invitation is extended to everyone—old and young—living in the house. If only an outer envelope is used, and single guests are permitted to bring dates, the envelope can be addressed to the person "and Guest." While traditional etiquette is uncomfortable with inviting unknown guests, the courtesy of encouraging unattached people to bring dates has led to this addressing convention. Outer envelopes must have return addresses on them (etiquette cares about the postal service as well).

- The *inner envelope* has only the names of the invited guests written on it.

STANDARD ENCLOSURES
- *Pew cards* (if guests will be assigned a specific pew during the ceremony in a house of worship)
- *Admission cards* (still used if the ceremony takes place in a house of worship that gets enormous amounts of foot traffic—think Manhattan's Saint Patrick's Cathedral)
- *Response cards* (see below)

- *Travel information* (directions and maps, lists of local entertainment, hotels, and other useful details)

WEDDING INVITATION LANGUAGE

- The *most basic invitation* to a wedding ceremony follows a no-frills informational pattern: The hosts request the honour of your presence at a marriage of the bride to the groom on a specific date, at a certain time and a particular place.

Mr. and Mrs. Harris Tweed

request the honour of your presence

at the marriage of their daughter

Maria Felicia

to

Mr. Andrew Brian Cabot

Saturday, the ninth of August

two thousand and eight

at four o'clock

Adam's Apple Orchard

RSVP

- *Extremely formal wedding invitations* are slightly different (and more labor intensive) in that one writes in the prospective guest(s) name(s):

Mr. and Mrs. Harris Tweed

request the honour of

Mr. and Mrs. Phillip Boyd's [these names handwritten in]

presence at the marriage of . . .

- *Enclosures with reception information* are used if those details will not all appear on the invitation (because the reception is being held at a different venue than the ceremony). Note that the name of the town is mentioned on the reception card, as it was on the wedding invitation:

Reception
immediately following the ceremony
Buttercup Club
2834 Market Street
Smumville

- *Invitations to the reception only* are phrased differently:

Mr. and Mrs. Paris Hat
request the pleasure of your company
at the wedding reception
for their daughter
Hanna Anna
and
Mr. Eric Carlyle
Saturday, the eleventh of November
at seven o'clock
The Explorer's Society
Fifty-four West Fifty-third Street
New York
RSVP

- *Invitations to the wedding and reception together on the same card:*

Mr. and Mrs. Tom Collins

request the honor of your presence

at the marriage of their daughter

Judith Linda

to

Mr. Milo Evans

Sunday, the tenth of February

at half after three o'clock

Sacred Heart Church

Middletown, Iowa

and afterward at the reception

The Grange Restaurant

RSVP

- *Invitations to the reception long after the wedding has happened:*

Mr. and Mrs. Fisk Johnson

request the pleasure of your company

at a reception

in honor of

Mr. and Mrs. Ernest Wilder . . .

- *If one forgoes response cards (one must indicate where guests may send their responses on the invitation itself):*

Mr. and Mrs. Clyde Clifford
request the pleasure of your company
at the wedding reception
for their daughter
Charlotte
to
Mr. Paul Pirrip
Wednesday, the tenth of September
two thousand and eight
at seven o'clock
The Madison Restaurant
New York
The favor of a reply is requested
975 Bedford Place
New York, New York 20008

* *Traditional language for host variations:*

  ° If the host couple (for the sake of argument, the bride's parents) is divorced, but both parents are hosting, each parent's name appears on a separate line. Ladies first, as usual:

  Mrs. Dinah Murphy
  and
  Mr. Bryce Mover
  request the honor of your presence . . .

° If one or both members of the host couple has remarried, one or both new couples are named:

Mr. and Mrs. Cowper Pine

and

Mr. David Fisk

request the pleasure of your company . . .

° If one of the bride's parents has died, the invitation can be composed listing only the surviving parent. If both parents are to be named, the format is different (titles are optional):

Rosalind Favor

daughter of

Bruce Finch and the late Ethyl Finch

and

Edwin Fleiss

son of Martha Fleiss and the late Bryan Fleiss

request the honour of your presence . . .

° If one of the bride's parents has remarried and the invitation needs to make sure everyone knows who the parent is:

Mr. and Mrs. James Remark

request the honor of your presence

at the marriage of her daughter . . .

° If the bride's parents have divorced and one has remarried but all parents are cohosting the wedding and want to be clear about who the parents of the bride are:

Mr. and Mrs. Jason Ravine

and

Mr. Patrick Pug

request the honor of your presence

at the marriage of the daughter of Mrs. Ravine and Mr. Pug . . .

° If the groom's family hosts:

Mr. and Mrs. Fletcher Willis

request the honour of your presence

at the marriage of

Miss Erika Foster

to

their son

Vincent Willis . . .

° If both sets of parents host:

Mr. and Mrs. Bert Foster

and

Doctor and Mrs. Jacob Santos

request the honor of your presence

at the marriage of their children . . .

° If someone else is hosting (and anyone can be listed as a host), substitute the line as necessary: "at the marriage of his daughter," "at the marriage of her sister," "at the marriage of their granddaughter," "at the marriage of their father," etc. (If the children of the wedding couple host the wedding, they are listed from oldest to youngest, bride's children first.)

° If the bride and groom host:

> *The honour of your presence*
> *is requested*
> *at the marriage of*
> *Miss Venice Burton*
> *to*
> *Mr. Carl Rottweiler*

OTHER ENCLOSURES

- *Response cards (optional).* Traditionally speaking, response cards should be unnecessary. Prospective guests are supposed to be able to get it together to write a quick note to their hosts, advising them of their plans to attend or not. A formal acceptance reply, whether written on a response card or a separate card sent by the guest, is almost a mirror image of the invitation, except that it is handwritten:

> *Mr. and Mrs. Jason Addams*
> *accept with pleasure*
> *Mr. and Mrs. Harris Tweed's*
> *kind invitation for*
> *December twentieth*

It is just as easy to give one's regrets:

Mr. and Mrs. Jason Addams
regret that they are unable to accept
Mr. and Mrs. Harris Tweed's
kind invitation for
December twentieth

- *Response card format.* Today, skipping the response card in hopes that people will get back to you of their own volition is the height of optimism. Keep looking on the bright side, and you'll probably only wind up having to telephone 89 percent of your prospective guests to shake answers out of them. Standard response cards ask only for the names of the people who will or will not be attending, and supply a "return by" date. The bride and groom or hosts generally provide the postage for response cards, except in the case of invitations being sent abroad.

M _____

accepts _____

regrets _____

The favor of a reply is requested by May 29

- *Additional enclosures.* Invitation packets often include information for traveling guests: a map of the area, a list of hotels, lists of restaurants and local entertainment, a discussion of other nuptial activities (if there are any), and any other details that might be useful for guests. They *do not* include information about wedding presents or wedding registries. It is just too mercenary to issue an invitation that comes with the demand for a present, as if one were making sure one's potential guests knew quite clearly that they will have to pay, in some way, for the honor of attending. Information packets can be sent with save-the-date cards or with the actual wedding invitations, depending on when that information is most useful. If guests need to make elaborate plans early, getting this information to them quickly is important.

Wedding Programs

- There is no standard format for wedding programs, and since programs are really not necessary, they can contain as much or as little information as the bride and groom want to include. Generally, the front of the program has "The Marriage of Bride's Name and Groom's Name" printed on it, above the date and the name of the venue. Inside the program, the wedding couple can thank family and friends, list the names of everyone who is participating in the ceremony, print the titles of the music pieces and hymn numbers and names of the performers, and list the readings and readers' names. If there are ceremony traditions that are novel, because they come from a different culture or because the bride and groom have invented them, this would be a good place to include any discussion or explanation.

Thank-You Cards

- Thank-you cards are blank cards that have the wedding couple's names on them. Traditionally, they should not have "thank you" printed on them, nor should they be fill-in cards (as in "Thank you for the _____.").

Wedding Announcements

- Wedding announcements are sent directly on the heels of the wedding, but *not* before. (Sending announcements before the wedding is asking for trouble, since they could be mistaken for invitations, and it looks odd to announce that something *has* happened on a date that has yet to occur.) Their traditional format is very similar to that of a wedding invitation.

Mr. and Mrs. Henry and Martha Ragsdale

have the honor of

announcing the marriage of their daughter

Daphne Anne

to

Mr. Pericles Jack Finn

Saturday, the sixth of September

two thousand and eight

Louisville, Kentucky

At-Home Cards

- This is an old tradition that has found a new use. For couples who lived apart until marriage, the at-home card was a good way for the wedding couple to let friends and family know their new address and contact information, and when they would be in residence (traditionally that date would be after the honeymoon). Today there is the additional benefit of letting people know what names the bride and groom intend to use after their wedding. These cards can be sent out with wedding announcements or thank-you notes, or they can be mailed solo. One format they could take is:

At Home

After February 29

Theodore White and Rebecca Settle

1710 Washington Market Drive

Lumberton, North Carolina 28358

(910) 555-4321

Twisting Tradition

This is a lot of protocol to swallow, particularly when you're gearing up to exercise your inner designer and want to have a little fun with your invitations. There is one primary rule of invitations, and of design generally, that should never be ignored: Be clear. Do not hide or muddle the important invitation details (who, what, where, when, how) behind your creative zeal. As detailed as the conventions above seem, other issues constantly rear their heads. So proceed with caution, and remember to proofread.

Invitations Are Not Film Credits

At the bottom of everything stationery-related, everyone needs to remember: (1) To everyone but the wedding couple and possibly their parents, wedding invitations are considered disposable, and (2) guests are not studying the invitations they receive to try to figure out who gave how much money toward the festivities. They just want to know when and where to show up.

This is not the place to make large statements about your relationships with your parents. However, when trying to decide whose names to include on the invitation, it is courteous and generous to name all of the parents as hosts (or at least offer to name them) if all of them contributed financially or were supportive in other ways. Talk to them about your plans ahead of time, since some parents may prefer not to be listed, even if they contributed. The worst course of action to take is to generate invitations and mail them, hoping that no one involved with financing the wedding will notice if names have been included or left out. They will notice and claim to be humiliated.

If you have paid for everything, can easily say you are hosting the wedding yourselves, and feel comfortable about not mentioning your parents in any way, you are of course free to leave them off.

When Do I Send Everything, Anyway?

Nuptial mailings do have a schedule, but in the hysteria to get everything out of the way, wedding couples often forget that timing is important. A general mailing protocol is:

- *Save-the-date cards:* Get mailed as far in advance as feels necessary. This can be six or eight months before the wedding if guests will need to book flights or hotel rooms in locations during high tourist seasons or for travel around national holidays or other peak travel times.
- *Wedding invitations:* Are mailed about six weeks before the wedding. There is some flexibility if the mailing is happening around holiday time (when the post office cautions that the mail takes a little longer to arrive) or if many invitations are being sent to guests who live out of the country. Timing can also be determined by when you need to get your RSVP information back.
- *RSVPs:* The easiest way to set the respond-by date (which will be included on the response cards) is to ask your caterer or venue coordinator how far

in advance he or she will need a final head count. Add an extra week or ten days to that date, to give yourself time to track down and harass people who have not sent back their response cards, and make that your respond-by date. (This is often around two weeks before the wedding.)

- *Wedding announcements:* Get sent right after the wedding, but not before. They can also be sent once the couple returns from the honeymoon.

- *Thank-you notes:* Should be dropped in the mail as soon as they are written, which should be as soon as possible after the present is opened and identified.

What If I Hate the Patriarchal Name Thing?

It is absolutely fair to hate the traditional construct where the wife's first name is dropped from the equation and she becomes "Mrs. HisName LastName," and there are ways to write people's names without embracing the format if it is objectionable to the sender. (Naturally, this applies only to couples where both people have the same last name. If married couples have different last names, their full names appear on the same line of the envelope being addressed.) You can also skip titles entirely, so that the names would look a bit less formal, as in "Barbara and Richard Motherwell," or you can use a longer construction that keeps the titles: "Mr. and Mrs. Richard and Barbara Motherwell."

Be aware, as you make your decision to drop the traditional construct, that as offensive as you find it, and as much as you would hate it to be used on your name, there are people who prefer it and find it comfortable and proper. Just as you would have them respect your feelings, try to take theirs into account. This does mean thinking a bit before putting pen to paper, but it is worth the effort. You don't have to be consistent in your envelope addressing style. No one will compare, and everyone will appreciate that you thought about your prospective guests enough to address them in a way that makes them happy.

What If He Took Her Name?

If you are addressing an envelope to a couple in which a man took his wife's last name, it is unlikely that they will embrace the traditional Mr. and Mrs. Man'sFirstName Man'sLastName construction. Follow the suggestions above and either drop the titles (Matilda and Gerald Clingfilm) or reorganize the names a bit (Mr. and Mrs. Gerald and Matilda Clingfilm).

Response Card Polls

Occasionally, people hope to gather quite a lot of information from their guests on invitation response cards, and they include various check boxes and polls. This is especially the case with menu choices. Before you start to worry about how to phrase the "salmon or beef?" question, make sure you actually need to ask. Guests notoriously change their minds about what they want in the weeks between the day they sent in their RSVP cards and the wedding reception, and caterers are often more than capable of planning food selections without this information.

If your caterer does, in fact, want to get food head counts, regardless of their questionable reliability, a line reading something like, "Please indicate if you would prefer beef, salmon, or a vegetarian option at the reception" would be appropriate. It isn't elegant, but neither is trying to figure out your gastronomic preferences two weeks into the future.

Communicating Desires

It remains a terrible idea to include registry information or any requests for presents at all on invitations. Convenience should take a backseat to graciousness, and it is just too demanding to issue an invitation along with something that is practically an admittance fee.

But I Want **Fun** *Thank-You Cards*

Well, who wouldn't? It is true that the standard thank-you card is rather uninspiring, but if you do opt for a more aggressive design, keep a few things in mind.

You don't want to wait on your stationery. One thank-you card concept, popularized by wedding magazines, is to have photos taken at the wedding of the bride and groom in full nuptial regalia holding cards that say "Thank You," and then using these images on the note cards. This sounds charming until you factor in how long it can take to get proofs and prints back from photographers—and then the cards still need to be printed up. By then there will be a huge number of thank-you notes to write, and the task will be overwhelming and your guilt levels will shoot sky-high. There are ways around the stationery delay, and there is nothing wrong with the idea, but the bottom line is this: The note matters more than the card you write it on.

Embracing Technology I: E-Invites

The e-mail invitation seems so promising, so clean and detached. It is environmentally polite (no trees harmed!) and modern. You can create an animated invitation or simple mass e-mail, and you can provide links that guide people seamlessly to your website or RSVP e-mail addresses.

So, where's the rub?

Well, e-mail, particularly mass e-mail, often gets caught in spam filters. People forget to check or automatically delete these carefully crafted e-missives. The older generation chafes at having to alter its ways and might not understand how to handle the brave new world of electronic communication. There is also something a bit impermanent about the electronic invitation, which may make prospective guests less likely to behave practically and actually take note of the important information (when and where the wedding will be, for instance).

Know your audience. If the bulk of your crowd would understand and be able to handle an e-mail invitation, go right ahead, but once you start second-guessing yourself and planning to do paper and electronic invitations, you may as well just count on the post office. People know what to expect when you go the paper route, and you'll have to spend fewer precious prewedding hours tracking down guests who either never got your invitation and are miffed or who thought they responded but actually didn't.

Embracing Technology II: Wedding Websites

Wedding websites fall under the heading of "helpful but not necessary." How useful they are really depends on how much information you have to tell your guests. Destination weddings are particularly good candidates for nuptial websites because of the amount of planning guests will have to do (finding hotels, making airline reservations, figuring out weekend activities, reserving cars), all of which can be made easier by referencing a regularly updated website.

Including registry information on wedding websites remains somewhat questionable. It is very hard to make pointed gift requests in a document—online or otherwise—that is otherwise a kind of invitation. If absolutely necessary (if, for example, you're faced with lots of overseas relatives with whom you don't communicate regularly and who are nagging your mother), you can list this information on a back page of the site, but whatever you do, don't broadcast it from the front page.

=========   *Etiquette in Action*   =========

WHICH NAME?

Dear Elise,

Is there a proper way to address an invitation to a soon-to-be-transgender person? My fiancé and I are friends with someone who lives as both a man and a woman and uses both names. Should we use the male name, female name, or both names on the invitation?

—Courteous

Dear Courteous,

You are right to wonder what your friend would want, and it is to your credit that you are so interested in everyone's feelings.

There is only one thing to do, and that is to ask your friend which of the two names s/he would like to use. Etiquette never requires mind-reading talents. You would only be doing everyone a service by quizzing your friend about what would make him/her happiest.

WRITING VERSUS PRINTING

Dear Elise,

Is it inappropriate to use printed address labels when sending out wedding announcements?

—Preparing to Mail

Dear Preparing,

Strictly speaking, all wedding correspondence should have handwritten names and addresses on envelopes. It is one of those old-fashioned stylistic courtesies that persist, in spite of technology. Wedding announcements generally get the same treatment as wedding invitations, so to fully embrace traditional etiquette, you would have to write your friends' addresses on the announcements, too.

Now, do people send out announcements with printed labels? It happens all the time and surely doesn't incur resentment. The printed labels look less formal and have a less personal, more "mass-mailing" feel to them. They aren't offensive, but they are a bit outside the norm.

SAVE-THE-DATE CARDS, INVITATIONS, AND THE LIKE: TWO QUESTIONS

Dear Elise,

I sent out save-the-date e-mails to all my guests six months in advance because we are getting married abroad. We also let everyone know about our wedding website, which has a lot of information and has an RSVP feature. Several guests have already RSVP'd online. If a guest has already replied online, should we send a formal invitation anyway? What if someone declines before the invitations go out? What if I send out formal invitations to people who have already given me a definite yes and they don't reply?

—Stymied

Dear Elise,

I hear it could be considered rude to send invitations to your guests more than eight weeks in advance of the wedding. Can you explain the rationale?

—Confused

Dear Stymied and Confused,

Wedding invitations should be sent to everyone who got a save-the-date notice. This means you must know how many people you can invite when you send out your save-the-date cards, because you can't give a lot of names the chop at the last minute without offending people. Do send invitations to people who indicated that they wouldn't be able to attend the wedding. People's plans change, and it is nice to keep them in mind. If you feel awkward about repeating the invitation, you can always include a little note with the invitation saying you just want to make sure your friends know they would be welcome. Finally, one should definitely send formal invitations to people who have already said they're coming. They will be expecting one, and you shouldn't count them as a "yes" until they RSVP to your actual wedding invitation.

Actual wedding invitations should contain a little more information, including the time of the ceremony and reception. Sending invitations early doesn't necessarily qualify as rude, but it can be counterproductive. People tend to forget about events that are planned very far into the future. Unless they have to travel (in which case you have no doubt already let your guests know about your plans via save-the-date cards), they really don't need more than six (or eight) weeks to make arrangements. At a certain point, too much advance notice just works against you—your guests will forget about your plans, and you'll be stuck calling people at the eleventh hour anyway.

Each piece of stationery exists to convey some piece of information. As long as you deliver your message clearly and in the right amount of time (for you and your guests), you'll be in great shape.

ADDRESSING A FORMER PRESIDENT

Hi Elise,

How would I address a wedding invitation to Bill and Hillary Clinton?

—He's Still My President

Dear He's Still,

There is a short answer to your question, and it follows the protocols of traditional etiquette, from which it seems foolish to deviate at this point.

Former presidents become "The Honorable," so you would be perfectly proper to address your invitation to "The Honorable William Jefferson Clinton and Senator Hillary Rodham Clinton" unless she has a title change in her career, in which case, adjust accordingly.

POSTHUMOUS HOSTING

Dear Elise,

How would you convey in a bridal shower invitation the fact that the bride's deceased mother is giving the shower?

—Organizing

Dear Organizing,

When you say the bride's deceased mother is "giving" the shower, do you really mean to suggest she is actually hosting (in the need-a-séance sense) or that the event is being hosted in her honor? It would look peculiar for an invitation to actually come "from" someone who is no longer among the living.

First, keep in mind that wedding shower invitations are usually issued on fill-in-the-blank informal cards, so there isn't always a need to be so formal. Now, if you would like to indicate that the shower is in honor of the bride's mother or being given by someone according to her wishes, there are a couple of routes you could take. As in the case of formal wedding invitations, one could include the deceased's name by writing "Bride's name, daughter of deceased's name" on the fill-in-the-blank card.

But you are clearly having invitations printed up, so the best bet would be to write something like:

Host's name
in honor of Bride's Mother's Name
requests the pleasure of your company
at a bridal shower for
Bride's Name
Date
Time
Place
RSVP

UNDELIVERED INVITATION

Dear Elise,

Someone just told me that a couple I invited to my wedding did not receive the invitation. How do I let these people know that they are invited and not a last-minute thought?

　　—Foiled by the Post Office

Dear Foiled,

By all means tell these people immediately about the mail snafu. In this case, the best thing for you to do is pick up the telephone and call your friends. Tell them that you heard that they had not received your invitation, that you absolutely want them to attend, that you're so sorry they didn't get it in a timely way, and that you hope they can still come to your wedding.

　　You don't have to turn yourself inside out apologizing, but a quick acknowledgment of their possible confused feelings should remedy the situation.

INVITATIONS, HOSTING, AND LANGUAGE

Dear Elise,

My husband and I are paying for most of our daughter's wedding. The groom's parents offered to pay for a few things (the music, the photographer, the bar). Would it still be proper to have only our names as the hosts on the wedding invitations and only have theirs under their son's as "son of Mr. and Mrs. X"?

　　—Composing Questions

Dear CQ,

Would it hurt your daughter's fiancé's parents if you didn't list them as hosts? Investigate this question. What you really don't want to do is create a situation in which the invitation language will come as a total surprise to them. In order to be clear, you may want to actually come up with a couple of different versions of the invitation language and let them see what you're considering.

It is acceptable, of course, to only list the bride's parents as hosts, or to list both sets of parents on an invitation, just as it is reasonable for the wedding couple to issue the invitations themselves, so what makes everyone happiest?

When you look at an invitation, do you really examine it to try to guess which members of which family spent the most on the wedding? Of course you don't. You look at the invitation to know who is getting married, when it is happening, and where you should be. So keep this in perspective. No matter what, you can be listed first on the invitation, but if it is important for your daughter's fiancé's parents that their names appear above his name as hosts in some way, consider being flexible.

There are no absolutes here. The point in all of this is to generate a welcoming invitation that doesn't trigger interfamily resentment.

Chapter 9

Asking, Giving, and Getting:
The Politics of Registries and Wedding Presents

Wedding presents inspire everyone's baser tendencies. They make us greedy or stingy (or at least make us think *others* are greedy or stingy). They inspire weird lapses of judgment ("everyone should give presents that cost as much as their reception meal"), desperate grasping at imaginary rules ("you have a *whole year* to write thank-you notes"), and bouts of social blindness ("I need money, so I'm going to include my bank account number on the invitation and make it easy for people to make deposits").

The standard parameters for wedding presents—both giving and getting—are quite clear and inflexible. They are constructed to protect everyone's feelings, not assist with the wedding couple's bank balance or ease the bride's writer's cramp. But that doesn't mean the wedding couple has no control at all over the gift giving.

Traditional Basics

- Guests are expected to give wedding presents if they attend the wedding and the reception. If they are invited only to the wedding ceremony, they are not obliged to give a wedding gift. (This is ancient tradition, stemming from the days of big, public, community weddings, which often happened in conjunction with much smaller, private receptions.) A wedding *invitation* alone is not a mandate to give a gift, especially if the invitee's connection to the bride and groom is tenuous. If family members or close friends are getting married, however, it is appropriate to send a present, even if one can't attend the nuptials.

- There are no rules about how much one should spend on a wedding present, and there never have been. One should purchase according to one's means, one's relationship to the wedding couple, and one's inclinations. If one cannot afford a present, a congratulatory card can be sent instead.

- In many cultures, it is traditional to offer cash. There are no limits, maximum or minimum, that one must offer. The gift is not meant to pay for the wedding. If checks are sent before the wedding, they are made out to the bride (using her maiden name). Checks sent after the wedding are made out to the bride or both the bride and groom using their married name(s).

- Presents are generally sent to the bride or to the bride's parents' home. Before the wedding, they are addressed to the bride using her maiden name. After the wedding, they are addressed to the couple using their married names.

- There is a persistent rumor that one has a year after the wedding in which to send a present. This is not really the case. It is best to give gifts relatively close to the wedding, either before or after, but there are no strict policies about timing.

- Appropriate presents: In the nineteenth century, guests who were not extremely close to the wedding couple were often discouraged from giving gifts at all, because to presume what anyone would like or need in the intimacy of his or her own home was considered impertinent. Such policies seem completely bizarre now that couples are able to make their desires known through (once utterly frowned-upon) wedding registries.

- Wedding registries offend practitioners of strict, traditional etiquette because they are blatant requests for presents and as such ignore the accepted pleasantry that gifts are purely the result of guests exercising their free will. It is very difficult to maintain this attitude now that wedding registries are so commonplace. As was the case with invitation response cards (see chapter 8, "In Print: Wedding Stationery and What to Write on It"), convenience and universality won out over tradition.

- One should never include registry information or pleas for cash or make any present requests (including "No gifts, please") on a wedding invitation. All of these details must be spread through word of mouth (tell anyone who asks, and let friends and family work their grapevines) and on wedding websites.

- It is wise to keep a record of all gift information: the date the present arrived, the name of the person who sent it, what the gift was, and the date the thank-you note was mailed. This will provide some protection against the inevitable: "Great-Aunt Dora never got a thank-you note for the cocktail shaker she gave you" complaints.

- It is appropriate but not necessary to give presents for second weddings. Often these gifts are more practical and less sentimental in nature than the choices for first weddings.

- The wedding couple does not have a year in which to write thank-you notes. Thank-you notes should be written as soon as possible after the presents have been opened.

- Traditionally, the bride writes all thank-you cards on stationery that does not say "thank you" on the front flap. It is completely reasonable for the groom to pitch in and write notes as well.

- The text of thank-you notes should be classy and not mechanical. It is good to include an acknowledgment of the actual present; with monetary presents one can make reference to the "generous gift" and indicate what the money has been earmarked for (i.e., yard landscaping, a down payment on a house, a fancy honeymoon meal).

- If the wedding couple fails to acknowledge a present after three months (in the form of a handwritten thank-you note), it is reasonable for the giver to ask if the present arrived.

- Even in the middle of the twentieth century, setting aside a room in which to display wedding presents was falling out of favor (though there is a great present-display scene in the 1950 movie *Father of the Bride*). However, if one must do this, one should display presents without cards to keep the givers anonymous, and organize the gifts so they don't demand comparison to one another (i.e., don't group all the bowls together). If checks are displayed, they should be arranged in such a way as to conceal the amounts.

- Present problems: Duplicate presents can be exchanged. Beware of returning gifts that come from close relatives unless they have specifically encouraged you to do what you want with them (people can be sensitive about these things, and it isn't worth triggering a fight—chances are you will know which gift-givers are the touchy ones). Broken presents can always be exchanged.

- If a wedding is canceled before it happens or is annulled immediately, wedding presents should be returned to the givers. If a wedding has been postponed, presents should be retained unless the postponement is really the beginning of the end for the wedding.

Twisting Tradition

Do these traditions seem harsh? Do they make it seem as if wedding couples are doomed to an avalanche of homemade cuckoo clocks and napkin rings shaped like mythical beasts? Are they overly prescriptive about what is an appropriate present?

Dealing with wedding gifts is like dealing with the weather. You can try to control your expectations and plan accordingly, but nature does what it wants to do. Ultimately, guests are people with opinions who will end up embracing or ignoring wedding registries according to their whims, and the bride and groom may have their hearts set on registering for items that their more traditional guests could find problematic. Everyone still has to be gracious.

What's Wrong with Registry Information on the Invite?

You've been cautioned against including registry information on the invitations, but you'll happily shout your gift choices to anyone who asks, so what's the point of the policy? The reasoning is elementary. Invitations have one very pure intention: They request the pleasure of someone's company or the honor of someone's presence. To combine an invitation with an explicit request for presents is to taint the purity of the welcome and turn it into an explicit exchange—"if you come, you have to give me something off this list"—and that seems rather mercenary. Keep these two things separate. Registries and invitations have nothing to do with each other. There are other ways to get your registry information out into the world (through the friends-and-family grapevine, on a wedding website, or through other casual communication with guests).

Money, Money, Money

Everyone needs cash for all sorts of reasons, and since you can use money to buy the things you want—things that would otherwise appear on a registry—the urge to ask for money seems in some sense reasonable. But just as love isn't rational, neither are expressions of enthusiasm, which is really what wedding presents are.

In some cultures, giving money is predictable and expected, and if you're a child of one of these communities or grew up in one of the places where cash gifts are the norm, you have every right to expect money from your family and the other people you grew up with. Of course, if your guest list is primarily composed of people who are not familiar with this tradition, you must be prepared to receive other kinds of presents.

No matter how practical or normal (in many communities) cash gifts are, however, actually asking for money is a delicate procedure. There is something cringeworthy about committing this pragmatic avarice to paper. If you're going to make the request, make it only in conversation and let it spread through word of mouth or by an informational page of your wedding website. You can use delicate phrases like, "We really have everything we need." If that doesn't quite do the trick, you can add, "But we are hoping to receive some money that we can put toward a house payment." If you can't bring yourself to speak this out loud, take your discomfort as a sign that you should absolutely not ask for money in print.

Of course, some people simply will always give money and others would never even contemplate doing anything so "impersonal." There is nothing you can do, beyond writing a gracious thank-you for whatever shows up.

The Swapping Scheme

Some couples, desperate to work the system, will try to exchange presents (for which they registered) for cash. This is an exhausting and rather cynical plan, even if they manage to find a store that will accommodate their hijinks. Inevitably, their scheme will be found out, much to the dismay of the people who wanted to give a carefully selected present, not cash. It seems harmless but is actually a case of trying to exploit a happy tradition (wedding presents) in the name of profit. The chances of this scheme coming back to bite the perpetrators vary, depending on how often the people who gave the gifts visit and how nosy they are.

Eloping and Presents

If you elope, do you get to register for wedding presents? If someone you know and love runs off and gets hitched in Vegas, are you obliged to give a gift? These may sound like "tree falls in the forest" questions, but elopements create a strange kind of pressure. If you elope, you can certainly register and let the details of your plans float around to all the people you didn't invite to your nuptials, and they can decide to give you a present or not. If you have a post-elopement reception of some sort, your guests will probably be more inclined to give a gift, but there are those who believe very strongly that people give up the "right" to expect presents when they elope.

When Do I Do What?

Timing plagues everyone. When should you send wedding presents? When should you open them? When should you deposit checks? When should you thank people? When should you start to worry that the post office filched your present before it got to the bride and groom? What should you do if your friends don't send a present?

There is one answer to all these questions: Don't stand on ceremony. Presents can be sent somewhat before or somewhat after a wedding. There's no point in waiting very long, although timeliness isn't crucial. Gifts should be opened as soon as they arrive, and thank-you notes should be written as soon as possible after you've figured out what the things are and who sent them. Checks should be deposited soon after they arrive, both as a courtesy so that the giver's checkbook will balance, and because there may be a timing issue. (As noted in Traditional Basics, checks sent before the wedding tend to be made out to the bride under her maiden name. If the bride changes her name to her husband's or takes an entirely new one, it can be difficult to deposit a check made out to her previous name.)

It doesn't really matter when you give your present. There's a persistent rumor that one has up to a year to give the wedding couple a gift, but that timeline is odd and really not mentioned in any traditional etiquette text. If you absolutely must send a present but are strapped and know you can't send one within a few months of the wedding, send a card, thanking your friends for the great time and the pleasure of seeing them get hitched. This buys you some time if you need it.

As a general matter, it is impractical to bring gifts to the wedding itself (though in some places and in some cultures, there are traditions for presenting presents at weddings). The problem is that the gift becomes something that the bride and groom have to cart off to someone's house or ship home before they go on their honeymoon, or otherwise deal with at a moment of High Distraction. It is much easier to give the gift when everyone isn't dancing or drunk or wondering why Uncle Todd isn't talking to anyone, when it will get the attention it deserves (and therefore doesn't get mauled or broken or left in a parking lot).

When to Inquire

When you send a wedding present out into the world and then hear nothing else about it, it is reasonable that you would be curious about whether your offering got lost in the mail or whether your friends are just being lazy about their thank-you notes. As a general matter, in cases like these it is considered fair to wait a few months and then gently ask the newlyweds if they have received the present. The key is to seem genuinely curious about the arrival of your present, and not churlish or scolding about not having received a thank-you note.

The same rules do not apply if you're on the other side of things. If some guests did not send a present or even a card, there is nothing you can do. It is unfair to prod or demand gifts from your guests. Maybe your friends didn't feel like giving one or couldn't afford one. The only exceptions to this are situations when a store or delivery company has told you that something was on its way but you haven't seen hide nor hair of it. Then you can ask, because some sort of information collapse is happening.

Weird Registries

Nowhere is it written that a wedding registry must contain appliances, linens, and fine china. Those may be the kinds of things deemed "necessary" by the Wedding Machine, but the registry field is wide open, depending on your needs and interests. You can register for camping equipment, plants from a local nursery, books, or fishing supplies. A bit of time spent with a travel agent could even help you generate a "honeymoon" registry. Be as bold or novel as you like. The possibilities are endless, and why not register for the things you really want? Keep in mind, though, that some people will not want to give you anything unorthodox, and you could still easily wind up with a cut-glass something-or-other or a blender.

Another popular choice is to register with charities so that guests can make donations in your name. This is wonderfully generous and commendable, but again, be aware that some guests won't want to participate in your plans. They may not care for the charity you selected, or they may want to get you what they feel is a "real" present. Ultimately, all you can do is make suggestions; your guests don't have to listen to you.

Really, No Gifts

One problem with the whole "no gifts" instruction is that no one believes you. Some guests will want to believe you but won't be able to make the leap of faith, and others will ignore the instruction as they would the ramblings of a lunatic. As a result, notations on invitations requesting no presents are trickier than not saying anything at all. The other problem with this request is that it will cramp some people's style. There are guests who will absolutely break out in hives if they can't give a wedding gift. Why trigger such inner turmoil in someone you're inviting to your wedding? A better policy is not to register anywhere, skip any invitation directives, and when people ask, tell them sincerely that you really don't want anything, but do not fight with them about it.

Of course, if you receive an invitation with this instruction, you really can take your friends at their word, and in lieu of a gift simply send them a card thanking them for being included in their celebration. You also wouldn't be wrong for not quite trusting your friends, and it is certainly not rude to check in with them to see if there is anything they would want, even an unorthodox gift. There may be extenuating circumstances that make presents problematic for them, and if nothing else, it would be interesting to hear what these may be.

=====   *Etiquette in Action*   =====

QUITTING, AFTER THE FACT

Dear Elise,

I have been married for only a few months, but I am filing for divorce. Is there a protocol about whether to return the wedding gifts when a marriage dissolves within a short period of time?

—Leaving

Dear Leaving,

You may be surprised to hear that, according to the protocols of traditional etiquette, you are under no obligation to return your wedding presents. Once the wedding has happened, even if the marriage is brief, you don't have to return a thing. It would not be expected.

If you really want to return your presents, you can, and include a note that says how grateful you are for their givers' support, but that the marriage wasn't built to last and you don't feel comfortable keeping the gift. You don't need to explain anything, though your actions will certainly trigger numerous questions. There is no pressure when it comes to the gifts, unless you feel that returning the items would somehow be therapeutic.

SAME MARRIAGE, TWO WEDDINGS, ONE PRESENT

Dear Elise,

I am invited to a church ceremony for a couple who already had a civil wedding months ago. I attended the "first" wedding and gave a present. Should I give another gift now?

—Again a Guest

Dear Again,

You really do not need to give multiple presents for the same wedding unless you are particularly moved to do so. It never hurts to send a card, so you can write one and feel virtuous if you like.

If that doesn't feel right (and there's no reason why it shouldn't), and you do want to make some sort of larger gesture, consider making a small charitable donation in your friends' names or offering them something amusing but not too financially taxing.

COMMUNICATING DESIRE THROUGH TRADITION

Hello Elise,

In Asian cultures, money is traditionally given to the bride and groom as a wedding gift. In America, it is common practice to give housewares and the like as gifts. If I had to choose, I'd prefer cash. Friends have told us to register for gifts anyway, and I signed up at a couple of places and listed them on our wedding website. Could I also list the name of my bank as one of my registries to hint at my preferences? Would that seem like I'm asking for money? Would it also be rude to "educate" people about the Asian custom of money giving on my website? I am not sure how comfortable I am with the idea of telling them in person.

—How Can I Say It?

Dear How Can I Say,

Indeed, many cultures, not only Asian ones, participate in money-giving wedding traditions. But present giving is something that people feel very strongly about, and it is as difficult to get cash cultures to switch to wineglasses as it is for bone-china types to hand over a check. Each present carries such different connotations for the gift giver that one could practically psychoanalyze your guests based on the presents they offer.

It is a sign that you can't bring yourself to tell someone out loud and in person that you want cash presents. Asking for money is an extremely uncomfortable thing to do, and your reluctance is completely reasonable.

Why is it acceptable to list your registry information and not a bank account number on your website? Well, in the first case, you're offering suggestions, but in the second, you are making a demand—for something that makes people feel squeamish.

You do not mention what percentage of your guests come from cultures where cash gifts are the norm, but in terms of explaining the cash tradition on your site, I'd caution against it for the same reasons outlined above. You are really best off letting the people who buy off registries check out your website and letting the cash-gift givers follow their own traditions. If people ask directly, and you don't feel too awkward, you can tell them you'd prefer money for a house payment.

TIMELY THANKS: TWO QUESTIONS

Dear Elise,

My fiancé and I have started receiving wedding gifts, and we want to start using these fantastic things. Can we use them before the wedding? Should we send thank-you notes right away or after the wedding?

—Presented

Dear Elise,

What is the time frame for writing thank-you notes for presents received at engagement parties and showers, and also for those received at the actual wedding (I assume more time is allowed for wedding presents because of couples being away on honeymoons)?

—Fêted

Dear Presented and Fêted,

In order to avoid becoming overwhelmed, the best plan is to write the notes as soon as you get the presents. This reduces the enormity of the task. Left to pile up, the notes become a gigantic obstacle that will give you a stomachache every time you pause to consider them.

The only true guideline for how much time is actually allotted is that notes should be written as soon as possible, which means they should be written as the presents come in. It is up to you whether you decide to use the presents or not. While the gifts got to you early, no one imagines you won't open them before the wedding, and nowhere does tradition hold that one must wait until after the wedding to open gifts. So write your notes now, and be glad you will have less to do after your wedding, when you will be craving nothing more than a break.

———

"NO GIFTS" VERSUS MOM

Dear Elise,

My fiancé and I want a very low-key wedding. That was all fine until my parents decided to throw a big reception in my hometown. I was thinking it would be a barbecue or something informal, but my mother decided to have it at a country club—exactly what we didn't want! We also don't want to receive gifts. My mother thinks it would be incredibly rude to print "No gifts, please" on the invitation and even thinks it is rude not to register. I asked if we could ask guests to donate to a charity instead, but she thinks that any mention of gifts at all is rude. What can I do?

—Foiled Bride

Dear Foiled,

Why don't you split the difference on this problem and tell your mother that you'll give up on your campaign to have "No gifts, please" on the invitations if she will get off your back about registering?

It isn't exactly rude to inscribe a "no presents" request on an invitation, but it is complicated, and it is certainly a violation of traditional etiquette policies to include any directives about presents at all on invitations. Your guests will find the command confusing (there have been episodes of situational comedies about this) or discomfiting (many people really would feel awkward about not offering a wedding present). Some people won't feel like giving you anything anyway, since this is, after all, a postwedding reception, and plenty of folks only feel inclined to give anything if they've been at the actual ceremony and reception. Really, this is a small point of concession. You aren't actively demanding anything from anyone, especially if you don't register.

Your mother, by the way, is mistaken about the rudeness of not registering. It is beyond acceptable to skip the registry entirely. And registries are not traditional at all—they are a contemporary convention that was utterly frowned upon when it began, which eventually became accepted. If anyone asks you where you've registered, you can sincerely say that you haven't picked out what you want because you really don't want anything at all.

This is not a battle about presents, at bottom. Clearly you and your mother are fighting for control over your wedding. Try to regroup and think of other ways you can salvage the informal quality that you want in your celebration. Maybe your parents could be persuaded to have a barbecue at the country club. Talk to your mother about this and drop the fight about wedding gifts. There's no reason to involve your guests in this struggle.

Chapter 10

Questions of Dress: From White Gowns to Wet Suits

"But I have nothing to wear!" is the delicious protest that follows so many invitations, wedding invitations especially. In an age of informality, the prospect of getting dressed up is rather daunting. Most weddings, after all, offer a set of sartorial challenges different from those of a night out on the town. No one wants to be the inappropriately dressed friend whose outfit becomes the joke of the month. Weddings are occasions where "Are you looking at me?" is probably not a paranoid question, in light of the fact that "all eyes should be on the bride."

Traditional Basics

The great advantage of traditions in dress is that, as with parochial school uniforms, everyone knows exactly what to wear. Strict protocols for formal dress don't permit extreme creativity, but they do stave off indecision, which for some can be much sweeter than all the freedom in the world.

Of course, the less formal a wedding is, the more flexibility one has. Marilyn Monroe, for instance, looked pretty stunning in the chocolate brown suit with a fur collar that she wore to her 1954 city hall wedding to Joe DiMaggio. But if you're in the mood to be rigorous, here are the ways to do it.

Brides

- The wedding dress needs little introduction. The volume and variety of styles fill the pages of countless bridal magazines every season. Brides can't go wrong with a white dress. Any kind of fabric in any shade of white is acceptable. The white tradition does not actually make any kind of statement about the bride's virginity, so no one contemplating white should take that issue into account. Dress style should be dictated by the location; weather; religious, cultural, and spiritual guidelines; and relative formality of the wedding.

- England's Queen Victoria is often credited with starting the white dress trend in the nineteenth century. She apparently chose the color because she felt it suited her, and there is something decadent and almost showy about the impracticality of white. It would be wasteful to choose it for an "everyday" dress that you could spill coffee on or otherwise muck up, so it makes sense to wear it on such an unusual and (with luck) unique occasion as one's wedding.

- Gowns are not required. Suits and dresses are also perfectly acceptable.

- Veils of any style are acceptable, particularly when they are part of cultural or religious traditions. It is interesting to note, however, that by the middle of the twentieth century, veils were considered a little bit dowdy and old-fashioned. In recent years there has been a fresh embrace of the veil. As with the dress, veil style should be determined based on the formality and the location of the wedding (trailing a few feet of tulle behind you down the beach isn't going to generate a flattering photograph, though you may pick up some crab legs and seaweed).

Grooms and Groom's Attendants

In a rare episode of turnaround, the rules for men's formal wear are much more complicated and rigorous than those for women.

- Formal daytime attire includes a morning coat (a full fitted jacket with two long "tails") or cutaway (a different fitted coat in which the front portion is shorter—jacket-length—and tapers back, so that the fabric sweeps back to one or two long "tails") with black or dark gray striped trousers; white shirt with a turndown collar; a bow tie; and a waistcoat (a white waistcoat is preferred, but it is so impractical that gray or black is acceptable).
- Semiformal daytime dress consists of a gray sack coat (a single-breasted jacket with a straight back), gray trousers (often striped), a white shirt, and a gray waistcoat.
- Informal daytime attire: A dark suit with a shirt (naturally) and tie is always appropriate. In the summer, a lighter-colored suit, or dark trousers with a white jacket, or white pants with a navy or gray jacket are also acceptable.
- Evening dress (tuxedos, tails) should not be worn during the day. The day ends at six o'clock in the evening, at which point you can hit the town in your finest finery.
- Formal evening attire consists of a black tailcoat and black pants, a white shirt with a wing collar, a white bow tie, and a white waistcoat.
- Semiformal evening attire includes a black tuxedo, all of the accessories that go with it, and a white shirt.
- Informal evening attire can include a tuxedo (especially if the bride is wearing a gown) or a dark suit.
- There are also men's formal dress variations that depend on region and season. In the South, for instance, the seersucker suit is a clean summer choice. These sartorial choices are very much local traditions.

- The fathers of the bride and groom usually take their wardrobe cues from the groom's choice.

- Ascot ties have been considered foppish for quite some time, but if you know what one is and believe you can pull it off, you certainly can go for it. This is an article of clothing often embraced by an older generation.

- If the wedding couple and their attendants are in the armed services, they may consider wearing their dress uniforms. If only the groom is in the military, he may wear his uniform, if his branch of the armed services permits it. Military policies for uniform wearing in civilian situations vary according to a number of variables, including whether the country is at war or not, so before making any final decisions, it is wise to consult with a military authority. If some members of the wedding party serve in the armed forces and some don't, you could have some in uniform and others in civilian attire, but it may be easier for the sake of symmetry to have everyone wear civilian dress. (Here, the decision does not have to be global—the groom's party could wear dress uniforms while the bride's attendants wear bridesmaid dresses if the wedding party breaks down that way.)

Bridal Attendants

As any former bridesmaid knows, the bride's attendants wear what they are told to wear. There are a few parameters that strict traditionalists follow.

- Bridesmaids all wear the same dress, though the colors can be varied. (This is quite a contrast to contemporary options. See "Twisting Tradition: Bridesmaid Variations" later in this chapter.) The maid or matron of honor often wears a dress that is similar to the ones the bridesmaids wear but distinct from them at the same time. (It can be a different color or a somewhat different style.)

- The bride can choose to outfit her bridal party in white. Traditionally, this was regarded as a bold but tasteful choice. Clearly it is contrary to everything we think about how only the bride wears white, but in this case, it would be her decision.

Mothers and Mother Types

So much thought has gone into what the mothers of the bride and groom should wear that bridal salons now feature whole "Mother of the Bride" sections. They are unnecessary, of course, because the mothers really can use their own judgment.

- General protocol permits long or short dresses for formal daytime weddings, evening dresses or cocktail dresses for formal evening weddings, and less formal dresses for daytime or informal evening weddings. Traditionally, slacks or pantsuits are discouraged.

- There is also a tradition of the bride's mother being the first to choose her outfit and then telling the groom's mother what she has selected so that the mother of the groom can make her choice accordingly. The two mothers' clothing does not need to match or be complementary in any way. Stepmothers should also be included in this discussion, if it happens at all.

- Black is acceptable, unless one of the mothers has decided to wear it as a way to silently state her feelings about the wedding. Signs that black is being worn in a negative way would include the refusal to smile and the addition of a heavy black veil. This should be discouraged.

Female Guests

Women are pretty much left to their own devices when it comes to deciding what to wear to weddings.

- One standard policy holds: It is not a good idea to wear a white dress to a wedding.
- There are also some general sartorial suggestions. For formal daytime weddings, cocktail dresses are a good bet (though all-black numbers are traditionally discouraged). Cocktail dresses can also be worn to semiformal daytime or evening weddings. Gowns or other long dresses can be worn to formal evening weddings. For informal nuptials, tradition favors dresses over pants.

Male Guests

Again, the men have a more prescribed dress code than women, which makes everything a bit easier.

- When in doubt, there is nothing wrong with a nice dark suit.
- For formal evening weddings, men can wear tuxedos or a black tailcoat with black trousers, white wing-collar shirt and tie, and a white waistcoat.
- Traditional attire for semiformal evening weddings is a bit complicated. One wears a black or very dark blue dinner jacket with matching pants, a white shirt, black bow tie, and a black waistcoat—or a good dark suit.
- Formal daytime attire is like that of the groom and his wedding party: black or gray cutaway coat, black or gray striped pants, gray waistcoat, white shirt, white tie.
- Semiformal or informal daytime attire is also a suit, though it does not have to be dark.

- If one is in the military, there are varying regulations about whether one may wear one's dress uniform to a civilian wedding. It would be wise to confirm with the armed forces authorities before skipping out in one's uniform.

Twisting Tradition

Once, the invitation alone was enough to tell a man whether he would need to have his cutaway jacket and trousers or his tuxedo cleaned and pressed, since location and time of day dictated an event's relative formality. Now dress protocol is practically a free-for-all—a celebration of personal style and individuality, where earlier it was a way to showcase how well one understood the protocols of one's surroundings, though this freedom does bring with it considerable confusion and indecision now that it is no longer obvious what one should wear. In fact, the tendency that people now have toward being extremely casual and despising any formality often creates friction when wedding couples want a fancy wedding and then have to worry that their black-tie event will be spotted with denim and sneakers.

Dress traditions are helpful crutches when one doesn't know what to wear, and it is always useful to fall back on them, but contemporary weddings can call for unusual attire, and even the people who live and die by sartorial convention would agree that practicality should not be ignored. One can always ask one's hosts what is appropriate to wear. There's no point in wearing five-inch heels to a scuba-diving-themed wedding during which the bride and groom will be wearing their nicest wet suits.

Women Wear the Pants

In the long and meticulous annals of wedding attire protocol, there is no mention of the possibility that women might want to wear trousers, let alone the question of whether or not they are acceptable. Anyone who has ever seen Marlene Dietrich in the film *Morocco* knows that a woman in men's formalwear can be something amazing. At the end of the day, if you dress well with respect for occasion and the bride and groom, there is nothing wrong with an elegant suit.

Really, White Isn't for Virgins

All of those sourpuss extended relatives can just swallow the nasty comments about the "real" significance of white, the implications of cream, and the hidden message behind ivory. White dresses have never been used to make any statements about the bride's anatomy or experience. Anyone who says anything to the contrary deserves an icy stare.

It is even acceptable for brides in the latter months of pregnancy—a time when one's virginity could not possibly be more in question—to wear white wedding gowns. There is, in fact, a growing industry in maternity wedding garb.

The fact is, the bride's sexual experience or lack thereof shouldn't be Topic A at the wedding, and what she wears isn't likely to offer up any clues worth exploring, anyway.

Bridesmaid Variations

Black dresses for the bridal party used to be verboten, but they are now permitted, especially since they allow everyone to entertain the idea (or delusion) that they are practical and will be worn over and over again at future cocktail parties or other such occasions. At least the color is generally flattering.

Another forgiving trend is for brides to vary the style of dress that their bridesmaids must wear, while keeping the color the same for everyone. This demonstrates a generous sensitivity to the likelihood that bridesmaids' body types will vary.

Of course, the most benevolent choice for a bridal party is for brides to relinquish control and encourage their bridesmaids to pick their own dresses. (This can be a free-for-all, or the women can be given general, minimal stylistic guidelines, i.e., tea length, evening gown, cocktail dress, navy, etc.)

Guests Aren't Psychic: How Do We Tell Them What to Wear?

All the careful work of traditionalists to let you know exactly what to wear when faced with all the shades of formality is useless if you don't know what sort of wedding you're attending. Classical formal invitations don't tend to indicate exactly *how* formal the wedding is, because in the past, the time of day and location of the events provided enough information for people to be able to get dressed with confidence. The reality, of course, is that today people get married at all sorts of times, and in places that don't really clue guests in as to what they can expect.

It is not necessary, but if you are nervous or if your venue has a strict dress code, you can indicate on the invitation that the wedding will be formal or informal. Another term that gets thrown around to describe evening affairs is "black tie"—which is synonymous with "formal" (men, get out your tuxes!). Putting any sort of dress directive on the invitation does not follow standard invitation protocol at all, but if you decide to include one, it would appear in the lower left-hand side of the invitation.

Of course, if you have a complicated wedding weekend full of entertainments and formality, you may want to include an actual insert, telling people to bring bathing suits for the afternoon inner-tube race, formal wear for the evening reception, and sportswear for the morning-after pre-brunch Pilates class. There is nothing wrong with giving people information that will help them pack (or shop and *then* pack) for your wedding. You could also provide minimal dress information on a wedding website, but tread lightly. You can't dictate everyone's attire. You're just giving a sense of the event so that guests can get dressed.

Obscure Instructions

Of course, some people go a little too far in their sartorial instructions, which can leave guests paralyzed in front of their closets.

Festive dress tends to mean nonblack clothing. You don't need to wear a feather boa or tuck a hibiscus blossom behind your ear or anything.

Black-and-white is a minitrend cribbed from Truman Capote's infamous 1966 ball. Guests are asked to dress in black and white and the décor is similarly monochromatic. Ideally, even here, women should make an effort not to wear all-white dresses to avoid appearing to compete with the bride.

Smart casual is a couple of notches below formal. This is a cocktail dress occasion if ever there was one.

Other themes, such as *Star Trek* or Disney or Renaissance or Goth, make the reception into something of a costume party. Everyone needs to be a sport, whether or not they get dressed up.

Inappropriate Outfits

A popular concern for brides is that someone (and there is usually a prime candidate) will decide to interpret "black tie" or "formal" as an excuse to break out the gold lamé or show off massive or newly acquired (or both) cleavage. The fear here is that the garish eyesore will be like a beacon that steers one's eyes away from anything attractive in the wedding photographs.

The only people whose sartorial choices you can command are the members of your wedding party. Beyond that, you're at the mercy of your guests' judgment. This doesn't mean you are doomed to singularly awful wedding pictures. If someone turns up in something truly distractingly hideous, you can take your photographer aside and instruct him or her to shoot around the problem outfit, while being sure to take a few requisite photos of the person for posterity.

If you are a guest and want to wear something outrageous, refrain. If you have just refurbished some part of your anatomy that doesn't usually see the light of day, or want to be extra sexy for your date, don't let it all hang out. There is always a way to showcase your assets while leaving something to the imagination. That is the best route to take, especially at a wedding.

Etiquette in Action

FEAR OF A RED DRESS

Dear Elise,

I have found the perfect wedding gown, but it is red. I know that my family will be shocked that my dress is the color harlots wear. They might even be furious and try to punish me if I pick this dress. But if I surprise them, that might anger them too. Which approach should I take?

—Wants to Wear Red

Dear Red,

You don't need me to tell you that you can wear anything you like to your wedding. But your family's feelings are important to you, and no one wants to deliberately create wedding strife.

Start dispelling the shock of the red at home. If you don't treat your color choice as lurid, you'll go far in diminishing people's angst. Bette Davis's character caused a scandal in *Jezebel* because she wore a red dress expressly to embarrass her date and enrage her hosts. Your choice reflects your taste, not a desire to be provocative. Set aside words like "harlot," and instead of surprising anyone, just confidently mention your dress and how happy the color makes you, and don't even give your relatives the opportunity to be childish, priggish, or apoplectic.

White dresses have not always been the norm anyway, and there are endless traditions and superstitions about what to wear at one's wedding, so if you find resistance, you can always point out that before the fad started in the nineteenth century, few people would have wasted their money on something as impractical as a white dress.

CLASH OF LOCALE AND DRESS CODE?

Hi Elise,

My partner and I are trying to figure out how formal we want our wedding to be. We're having a pretty large affair outside, with the reception in a tent. We are going to wear standard wedding attire (dress, suit).

Many of our friends are camping out for the weekend. They will also have a pool to use. We want everyone to be comfortable, but we don't want them in jeans at the wedding, and we want to let people know that they should bring swimsuits. How should we word the invitation?

—Dress Code Question

Dear Dress Code Question,

If your guests are actually camping out, you realize you can have only limited expectations of how formal and unwrinkled they will be at your event.

Traditionally, guests would understand what to wear to weddings based on what time and where the wedding events were scheduled to unfold. Clearly the ground has shifted, and in your case, you really might want to provide some direction.

What would you like to do? Would you like to tell your guests to dress up, but not too much? If your feelings about dress code are nonspecific, you may want to just include a note about what guests should bring with them in your invitation packet. You can mention here that they can bring bathing suits for the daytime activities and indicate that dress for your wedding is semiformal (if that description does it for you).

MILITARY DRESS FOR CIVILIANS?

Dear Elise,

What should a woman wear to a wedding for two military officers held in a navy chapel at noon in the summer? We were told that "tea length would be appropriate," but what about color? Do women traditionally dress in lighter shades in the summer, or would it be better to wear something dark because of all the uniforms? Should men wear dark suits? What should our daughter wear?

—What to Wear

Dear What to Wear,

As civilians attending a military wedding, dress options are really wide open. You don't have to worry about matching your outfits to the military uniforms, which leaves you with the standard question of what to wear to a summer wedding (you don't mention whether it is formal or not).

A "tea length" skirt or dress has a hem that hits substantially below the knee—midcalf or a little lower. As for colors, women should stay away from white. Many people are wearing black to weddings now, but in more traditional circles it still carries some negative connotations. Pastels are pleasant, especially for children, but since they aren't universally flattering, know that navy blue is a formidable wedding standby color. The choices are somewhat easier for men, who can opt for sober suits that may be waiting in their closets anyway.

WHETHER TO WEAR WHITE

Dear Elise,

I know you should never wear white to a wedding, but does this apply to other wedding events? Would it be inappropriate to wear white to a summer engagement party?

—Wondering

Dear Wondering,

The protocols for white shift around, especially now that the fashion cognoscenti are throwing all sorts of white outfits our way, convincing us that we won't pour berry desserts into our laps.

You are right that one really shouldn't wear white to a wedding unless one is the bride. The engagement party is a different story. While there are no specific rules about dress color at engagement parties, you are wise to be concerned. You know the bride and surely have an idea of how sensitive she is. If you are at all worried that she would react badly, wear something else or ask her ahead of time. Even if there is no "rule" that would be dented or broken, why not follow your instincts? Some people care very much about these things; others wouldn't even consider them worth a thought.

FASHION CLASH

Dear Elise,

My fiancé says he will only wear jeans to our wedding. He says he just doesn't feel comfortable in any other pants. I am wearing a full ball gown. I would like for him to be himself and still be dressed up special for the occasion, so we don't look mismatched at our wedding.

—Punk Princess

Dear Punk Princess,

There are plenty of sartorial rules of etiquette for formal weddings, but all you really want to know is how to make your fiancé presentable.

Are you having a collision of philosophies? Does he know how important it is to you that he wear something more formal than jeans? If you've discussed this and he is still clinging to denim with no compromise in sight, you're probably best off embracing the probability that you will be wearing a ball gown and he will be in jeans, and perhaps you can embrace the "high/low" aesthetic. He knows how he wants to look for his wedding, just as you know how you want to look. The best thing you can do is accept each other's choices, and as long as they are made with respect for the wedding and for each other, you're in good shape.

ALTERATIONS

Dear Elise,

My future mother-in-law gave me her mother's wedding dress. It's great, but I want to modify it. My mother thinks this would be insulting, but my fiancé's mother told me to do anything I want. Who is right?

—Perplexed

Dear Perplexed,

Your mother is nervous. This is not really about the dress. Your fiancé's mother gave you permission to go to town on the dress. Any traditional etiquette text would tell you that you are now free to do what you want with it. Still, humor your mother and pick up the phone. Ask your fiancé's mother point-blank if it would be all right for you to make significant alterations. If she doesn't flinch, trot back to your mother and tell her to find something else to fret about.

All you are doing is a bit of due diligence. If you tell your mother that she's nuts, you'll only set the stage for more angst, to which she'll add the complaint that you don't take her seriously. So have a nice chat with your fiancé's mother and congratulate yourself on diffusing maternal ire.

COLOR CAUTION

Dear Elise,

Is wearing black to a wedding (or wedding events like a bridal shower) a big no-no? I always thought black conveyed elegance, but I've had several people tell me that it is inappropriate to wear black to a wedding or related events. Are there any rules of etiquette concerning this?

—Unsure of Attire

Dear Unsure,

There are plenty of ideas about black and weddings, though you must decide for yourself how to interpret them. All of these notions apply to weddings only, and not to the events that surround the nuptials.

The standard hard line is that one should never wear black to a wedding because of its connotations of mourning. Some go so far as to imply that wearing all black either imparts bad luck to the bride and groom or speaks volumes about the black-wearer's attitude toward the wedding. (You should note that clothes with black in the pattern do not fall under this caution.)

These are the rules of tradition that many people happily break.

Brides even frequently outfit their bridesmaids in black. For the most part, you should be perfectly fine wearing black to a wedding. If you feel nervous and this is a traditional crowd, you might be more comfortable in something nonblack. Now that you know the lay of the land, the rest is up to you.

PROPER TRAINING

Dear Elise,

My fiancé and I are getting married in the tropics, but the dresses I like best have cathedral trains. This is my second marriage. Is it true that brides in their second weddings shouldn't have long trains? Is a cathedral train too long? Would a dress with a train be inappropriate for a beach wedding?

—In Training

Dear In Training,

You're looking for rules where they have become somewhat extinct. Today everything is permitted as far as wedding dresses go, even for second weddings.

Don't believe so-called traditionalists who would advise restraint and urge you not to wear a formal gown. The people inclined to make such comments would be most excruciatingly rude for trotting out memories of the unfortunate past on a happy occasion. While you can wear anything you like, take a moment and think about how your dress will look in your venue.

"Cathedral-length" trains—several yards of material cascading down from the waist—make for extremely formal wedding gowns. How would you feel walking on the beach with all kinds of fabric trailing behind you? It may be impractical, heavy, and ultimately something that just feels weird out in nature, even if it is appealing in the store. If you are absolutely sold on both the dress and the beach, you can bustle the train, which may help with any awkwardness.

You want etiquette to give you guidance, but at the same time you want confirmation of your inclinations. My advice is practical as well as romantic. Your dress will have to travel, and the more fabric you have to deal with, the more chance there is of wrinkling or staining. Just as you wouldn't wear white velvet in the Caribbean, you also might not be inclined to drag five or ten extra pounds of train behind you.

PAGING MISS HAVISHAM!

Dear Elise,

My daughter's fiancé's mother just showed her the gown she intends to wear to her son's wedding. It is, without a doubt, a wedding dress (off-white, satin, strapless, the whole deal). My daughter is very upset. Is there anything I can say? Should my daughter's fiancé talk to his mother and get her to wear something else?

—Appalled

Dear Appalled,

This is, indeed, tricky. As a general matter, you should stay far, far away from any conversation with your daughter's future mother-in-law about what she intends to wear to the wedding. She almost certainly knows that she's doing something wrong and will respond poorly to being told that her choice is inappropriate. The only person who is in a position to say anything about her sartorial choice is her son. If he can stand up to her, he can tell her that he is uncomfortable with her wearing a wedding dress to his wedding.

Of course, her decision to wear a wedding dress to anyone else's wedding—let alone her *son's*—is completely ridiculous. (I will also here gently restrain myself from elaborating on any of the creepy Oedipal implications behind her gesture.) What reasonable person would decide to do that, unless she is deliberately trying to be provocative? Your daughter should not take the bait. Her mother-in-law-to-be may be hoping to get a big reaction out of her, and there's no point in rewarding her.

The best course of action for you and your daughter will be to assume a mask of polite detachment. If your daughter's fiancé fails to convince his mother that this dress is a mistake, and she does wear it, there is only one person who will come off looking insane and weirdly competitive at the wedding.

Your daughter should also have a word with her photographer about coming up with a plan for acceptable pictures, but beyond that, she can take comfort in the knowledge that while no one would blame her for her future mother-in-law's dress choice, everyone will think she is remarkably brave to join that woman's family.

With any luck, someone will pour a hefty glass of red wine in the woman's lap, but even if that doesn't happen, no one, no one at *all*, will be confused about which woman is the bride.

Chapter 11
The Last Supper: The Rehearsal and the Rehearsal Dinner

Unless the bachelor or bachelorette events are held immediately before the wedding (something that tends to be discouraged, for reasons of propriety and practicality—no one wants to deal with incredibly hungover, green-turning brides and grooms, barely able to tolerate the volume of the officiant's voice), the rehearsal and rehearsal dinner kick off the nuptial festivities. What exactly happens at a wedding rehearsal, and is one even necessary? What are the rules about the dinner? It all depends on how much control you need to have, how strictly you plan to follow a traditional path, and, of course, what you want.

Traditional Basics

Traditionally, wedding rehearsals are recommended for anyone who is doing anything more complicated than having the bride and groom just show up at the altar.

The rehearsal is typically held the afternoon or evening before the wedding in the wedding location (it is a good idea to try to reserve a rehearsal time at the same time one books the wedding venue). If the space isn't available for a rehearsal, then the wedding party and officiant can be assembled elsewhere, and the aisle length and altar width approximated (someone efficient should take measurements ahead of time for this).

Everyone participating in the wedding ceremony should attend the rehearsal if possible: the wedding couple, the bridal party, whichever parents of the wedding couple are taking part in the ceremony, any readers the couple may elect to have, and the officiant. In addition, if there are complicated music cues or if the speed of the music needs to be worked out, and it isn't prohibitively expensive, it can be a good idea for at least one of the musicians (if any have been hired) to attend the rehearsal.

Ideally, the rehearsal is held at a discreet hour that doesn't interrupt work schedules. The whole affair should not take more than an hour to sort out.

Extreme traditionalists will have the bride "direct" the rehearsal but not participate in it, for fear of bringing on bad luck. (What the threat is tends to be left to the imagination.) Instead she casts a friend or relative to be her stand-in for the walk-through. (This superstition is taken more seriously in some regions than others.)

The actual ceremony does not need to be rehearsed. The rehearsal is really an opportunity to figure out the order in which everyone should walk down the aisle, resolve timing issues (how fast the processional should be played, the speed at which the wedding procession should walk down the aisle, the pace of the postceremony retreat from the altar), and give any children in the wedding party a chance to get comfortable with what they'll be doing.

One standard processional pattern can be found in the Traditional Basics section of chapter 12, "Ceremony or Talent Show: Vows, Readings, and Performances." A generic recessional pattern can be found in the Traditional Basics section of chapter 12 as well.

The rehearsal dinner is traditionally the groom's family's arena. The groom's parents host the meal as a courtesy to the bride's family (who, traditionally, shoulders the burden of the wedding).

The dinner can take any form. It can be formal or informal, and it can happen in a restaurant or country club. It can be a backyard barbecue, a cocktail party, a buffet extravaganza, or a sit-down banquet with multiple courses.

There are several gambits for traditional rehearsal dinner guest lists:

The most exclusive rehearsal dinner guest list includes only the immediate families of the bride and groom and their spouses or partners, the wedding party and spouses or partners, and the officiant (particularly if he or she helped with the rehearsal) and his or her spouse or partner. Small children in the wedding party are not required to attend the rehearsal dinner.

A more inclusive guest list includes all of the above and adds all relatives who have come to town for the wedding and their spouses, and friends who have come from out of town for the wedding and their spouses. The key, as always, is to be consistent. One can't invite only one's favorite aunts or exclude the handful of distasteful spouses of friends.

Rehearsal dinner invitations can be formal or informal. They can be pre-printed invitations, but fill-in cards or handwritten notes are also common. Guests can even be invited casually via telephone calls or e-mails.

Seating at rehearsal dinners can be another opportunity for people to jockey for attention and try to find slights where none were intended. One standard seating scheme—for a long rectangular table—looks like this: The bride and groom sit beside each other (bride on groom's right) with the best man on the bride's right and the maid or matron of honor on the groom's left. The dinner's hosts (traditionally the groom's parents) sit at either end of the table, and the mother of the bride takes the seat to the right of the groom's father, while the father of the bride sits on the groom's mother's right. The rest of the seats are filled by the officiant (and his or her spouse), grandparents, and other members of the wedding party. (Divorced or separated couples should not be seated near each other, and ideally would be seated at different tables.) Clearly this seating applies for large tables. Other seating arrangements are also acceptable.

What happens at a rehearsal dinner besides eating? Toasts! The groom's father, as host, usually makes the first toast to welcome everyone, and the bride's father gives a toast in response. Then the wedding couple often takes the opportunity to toast their parents and give presents to the wedding party, then the attendants and other guests can jump in with toasts. The bride and groom can also insist on the toasts being made in the order they prefer. Dancing is not required.

Twisting Tradition

Because there are few codified rules for the rehearsal and rehearsal dinner—and the few that exist mostly derive from practical issues—there aren't that many traditions that need to be remembered or debunked. The problem that contemporary people run into more than anything else is that there really isn't that much protocol, so the key is to fall back on standard policies of politeness.

Rehearsals Aren't Universal

If you don't need a wedding rehearsal, you don't have to have one. They are primarily useful if you have a lot of people, aisle choreography, readings and performances that you need to put in order, and young children who need to get comfortable with their jobs. If you are planning a simple ceremony with few people and minimal action and you aren't worried about planning out every footstep, a rehearsal may not be necessary.

And even if you don't have a rehearsal, you can still have a rehearsal dinner.

Anyone Can Host

Rehearsal dinners: They're not just for the parents of the groom anymore. The tradition of the groom's parents hosting is an expression of courtesy because the bride's family typically paid for everything else wedding-related. Increasingly, wedding costs are being split in all sorts of ways, with the wedding couple often footing the bill entirely.

The bride and groom can host their own rehearsal event. A friend can step in and do the honors too, as can other relatives, or the whole thing can be a collaboration with the bride and groom and their families, as so many weddings are.

Dinner Is Not Necessary

It may be called a "rehearsal dinner," but you don't have to actually rehearse anything, if you don't need to, and you don't have to serve dinner. Dinners can be expensive and bring on all kinds of dilemmas: "I can afford to pay for a delicious three-course sit-down meal for twenty, but that means I can't invite any of the people I actually like!"

In lieu of a formal dinner, you can have a casual backyard barbecue or meet at an inexpensive restaurant. If you want to maintain a more "sophisticated" edge but can't swing the whole meal, you can have a cocktail party, where you need to serve only drinks and hors d'oeuvres. If you go the cocktail route, be sure to let people know on the invitations that this is a cocktail party, and try to time it so that people are not likely to show up expecting dinner.

If these possibilities seem too stodgy, there are still more choices, depending on how many people you have on the invitation list and whether or not the hosts have strong feelings about this being a traditional affair. You could gather to hear live music, spend an evening bowling, trundle the crowd along for a bar crawl, have a wine tasting, play poker—anything is possible as long as the key players are willing.

Invitation Caution

Everyone has to know his or her limitations, and it doesn't matter if the boundaries are a result of space or money constraints or a social anxiety disorder or any other possible issue. Limits are reasonable. But they must be handled well. This means:

- Everyone in a category must be invited, from both sides of the aisle. You can't invite the groom's aunts and not the bride's. You can't invite the only grandparent who doesn't annoy you and leave the others to fend for themselves. It is all or nothing.

- Significant others should be invited, especially if they've come from out of town. It is just awful to show up in a strange town and then be deserted in a hotel with only the television and minibar for company.

- There will inevitably be some guest list give-and-take. As is the case with the wedding guest list, it doesn't matter if the groom's family is much larger than the bride's. The event isn't a popularity or breeding contest. It is crucial, however, that no one take advantage of the hosts. If the hosts can afford a huge bash, then they are entitled to throw one, but they should make every effort to accommodate the interests and guests of the other interested parties. On the other hand, if the bride and groom desperately want a small rehearsal, the hosts should listen to them and seek a compromise. This is not the place for everyone to get cranky and start beating their breasts over a "fantasy rehearsal dinner."

- Children do not have to be invited, and all the policies about consistency apply: If one niece is invited, all the nieces and nephews should be included; if one first cousin gets the call, all the other first cousins need invitations. To do otherwise is to invite endless strife and whining. If you exclude children, particularly those of parents who come from out of town, prepare for complaining and absenteeism. You aren't doing anything wrong, but people will whinge about not having child care, not wanting to leave their children with strangers, and any other issues that seem unreasonable to people with no children and obvious to people who do have them.

Etiquette in Action

WHEN GUESTS ARE TOURISTS

Dear Elise,

Our wedding is in my hometown. My fiancé's family is from far away, so my family suggested having the rehearsal dinner at a local tourist attraction. We are paying for the wedding ourselves and can afford to pay the entrance fee to the location for the wedding party, but we'd also like to invite extended family and out-of-town guests. Is it acceptable to ask them to pay their entrance fee themselves, since this a fully optional event on their part?

—Tourist Attraction Bride

Dear Tourist Attraction Bride,

Generally, if you invite people to a structured event like a rehearsal dinner, you should pay for them. In this case you would be obliged to pay for your guests' entrance to the dinner party (if that is what you are having) and, of course, the meal.

On the other hand, if you are doing something very casual—a drop-in, unstructured affair—where the tourist attraction is something that people have an option of visiting on the side, you would not be as responsible to pay for everything. Your obligation in this case really depends on what you are planning to do. Is this a group excursion with dinner, or are you just letting people know what their entertainment options are?

If you are juggling finances and do want to invite a lot of people, consider having something like a cocktail party instead of dinner. You could save money on food and seating and use that cash to pay for more people's entrance to the tourist site. (I'm sure you've also thought of this, but you could also look into getting a reduced group rate for admission to this tourist attraction.)

SOLICITING MENU CHOICES

Dear Elise,

My son is getting married, and my husband and I are hosting the rehearsal dinner. We were planning on offering a choice of dishes at the rehearsal dinner. I heard that it is "tacky" to offer a choice on the reply cards we send with invitations, but I thought that it was gauche not to offer meal options.

—Confused

Dear Confused,

Reaching back into the annals of etiquette, there is scant mention of offering menu choices on response cards. Some of this comes from the fact that until quite recently, response cards themselves were considered horribly gauche.

The world has shifted, and these days response cards are expected because in fact, very few people now realize that they are supposed to respond to invitations without prompting and pre-addressed envelopes. Menu choices on response cards, however, is a more recent phenomenon—the result of people needing to plan everything minutely; guests needing to have their dietary issues taken care of; hosts wanting to be as gracious as possible while maintaining a lot of control. It isn't actually necessary to secure your guests' meal choices in advance unless you, your caterer, or the restaurant you're using desperately requires this information. At bottom, it is awkward to solicit meal choices, and the information you collect is often unreliable, because people inevitably change their minds. But if you have to gather this information, you aren't being rude. To suggest that you are is offensive, in and of itself.

REHEARSAL DINNER GUESTS: THE COUSINS

Hi Elise,

My parents are hosting an elaborate wedding weekend, while my fiancé's parents are hosting only the rehearsal dinner, and I wonder how I should handle the guest list for that event. My fiancé's parents have already indicated that they'd like to keep the number of attendees rather low.

We have many out-of-town guests, including two of my cousins, who are playing our ceremony music. Should I ask my fiancé's mother if my cousins could be invited to the dinner? Should I ask if my cousins' boyfriends could also be invited? I don't want to be rude.

—Stranded

Dear Stranded,

If your fiancé's parents are hosting the rehearsal dinner, they will have control over the guest list. While this means that they may tell you that they can't accommodate any extra guests beyond the bare minimum, you should indeed ask them if they could invite your cousins and their boyfriends. Your instincts are quite right. Since they have traveled for your wedding and are participating in your ceremony, your cousins should be invited, with their boyfriends, too, since they are your cousins' committed partners who have also traveled for the wedding.

Be diplomatic. Ask if you could add your cousins and their boyfriends to the guest list. This is one of those "nothing ventured" situations. Your future in-laws may have only the smallest idea that your cousins exist, so asking after your relatives' interests is certainly not rude. If your fiancé's parents refuse, you will have done your best, and you and your family can perhaps come up with something else for your cousins to do.

DRY REHEARSAL

Hi Elise,

My fiancé's family is full of binge drinkers. This is something he has lived with all his life and he (and I) would prefer not to see it on his wedding day. My family does not drink at all and would be appalled by their behavior.

We decided not to serve alcohol at our wedding reception, but his family wants to host our rehearsal dinner. I understand that the hosts should be allowed to determine what sort of party they're throwing, but how can I politely let them know we don't want alcohol served? Their behavior will be embarrassing. These people think nothing about hopping behind the wheel of a car after they've "tied one on," and I could never live with myself if there were an accident because of a party in our honor.

—Worried About Wine

Dear Worried,

One of the most difficult lessons to learn in planning a wedding is that you can't control everyone. It can be incredibly frustrating. This is just to prepare you for the worst.

You can take some steps to protect your interests. While there is no way to be subtle about your desires, you can make gentle requests of your hosts. One cowardly but effective approach is for you (or your fiancé) to say that your family has requested that no alcohol be served for religious reasons. It's worth a shot, but your fiancé's family may not want to be so accommodating, and there is only so far you can dictate to your hosts what kind of party they will throw.

If you are seriously concerned about drunk driving, you may want to seek the assistance of the restaurant and see if they have any policies in place about how to ensure that people won't hit the road fully tanked. If the venue has hosted a rehearsal dinner before, this will surely not be a novel concern for them. You may also want to extend yourself further and gather information about shuttle buses they can hire to transport revelers to and from their hotels.

PARENT PRESENTS AND HONESTY

Dear Elise,

I attended a wedding rehearsal dinner where the bride and groom gave presents to the whole wedding party and both sets of parents. Is this an expected ritual? My parents have been extremely generous and helpful (financially and emotionally), but my fiancé's parents have been the opposite.

It is important to me to do something really nice for my parents, but I am much less inclined to do so for my fiancé's parents. I plan to get them both something, but I am worried about having to present two disparate gifts in front of people at the rehearsal dinner. Is it wrong to not treat both sets of parents equally, and should I present the gifts at the rehearsal dinner?

—Torn

Dear Torn,

Weddings contain plenty of traditions, few of which are necessary for happy nuptials. There are many opportunities for the wedding party and family members to receive presents, and it is certainly not necessary to give these gifts in front of an audience. Weddings do not have to be award ceremonies. So before you get too attached to the idea of giving presents at your rehearsal dinner, decide if you want to make grand public gestures or if you would be better off giving your presents under more discreet circumstances.

Unless you feel comfortable giving both sets of parents presents in the same spirit, you are risking hurting and humiliating your future in-laws. In spite of your negative feelings toward them, do you really want to be on record for doing something in front of an audience that will surely alienate them?

You don't have to give your parents and future in-laws the same presents or presents at all. If you choose private moments either before or after the wedding, you can be as lavish as you like with your parents, and your fiancé's folks never have to feel slighted. You can always give a general "thank you" toast at the rehearsal or postwedding reception. Do yourself a favor, though, and don't stir the pot. With families, trouble may always come looking for you, but there's no need to welcome it.

RESCUING THE REHEARSAL DINNER

Dear Elise,

My fiancée's family is well-off. From the get-go, my parents have accepted their "responsibility" to throw us a rehearsal dinner, but now we're confused. Most of our friends and relatives will be coming from out of state. We're expecting about 150 people at our wedding and reception. My fiancée feels that *all* of her friends, her family's friends, etc., should be invited to our rehearsal dinner, while my mother has graciously set a limit on the number of guests she can afford to host. My fiancée thinks my mom is being "cheap" and that she should get to invite whomever she wants. I don't want to start any more arguments. How can I keep the peace?

—Rehearsal Struggle

Dear Struggle,

You must feel you're caught in the crossfire.

No one hosting any wedding event is under any obligation to bankrupt him- or herself in the interests of providing some happy event for the wedding couple. Perhaps your fiancée doesn't understand that it isn't a question of cheapness or wanting to rain on anyone's parade, but of basic resources.

What can you do? First, there is no need for this party to be a dinner, if feeding so many people multiple courses is too taxing. Everyone must learn to be flexible. Your future wife and her mother must be willing to narrow their visions of this party, or consider contributing to the rehearsal dinner finances, and your family should try to be more flexible about head count, while sticking to the budget.

There is no point in everyone getting resentful. The difference in your parents' resources seems to be no secret and no surprise. So now you, your mother, your fiancée, and her mother, faced with the facts, must compromise. It may not be what everyone had in mind, but you can create a highly entertaining, inclusive event, which is what you all want anyway.

SISTER-IN-LAW PITCHES REHEARSAL?

Dear Elise,

My brother's fiancée wants a traditional wedding, financially speaking, where my husband and I would pay for the rehearsal dinner (our

parents really can't help at all). I agreed to host a barbecue at my
house. Unfortunately, my brother's fiancée wants the rehearsal dinner
to be held at a fancy restaurant and wants us to pay for it. I don't have
the finances to cover this, and why should I be expected to take on
this burden? My brother says that her parents are getting mad that his
family isn't paying for anything. What can I do?

—Angry Sister

Dear Angry,

No one likes to be bullied, especially not in the so-called name of
tradition. First you must realize that, even if you were the mother of
the groom, no one would arrest you for not accommodating the bride's
wishes. You were asked to throw a rehearsal dinner, and you've offered
to host a party that you can afford, and that's all that is required of you.

I don't know where the bride, her family, and your brother
learned what is and is not "traditional," because they certainly didn't
develop this idea from reading standard etiquette texts or being
considerate. It really is not up to anyone to dictate the conditions of
the rehearsal dinner if they are not paying for it. They can make some
requests, of course, but fundamentally this is your present to the
bride and groom and that's that.

What do you do? Be firm. Tell your brother that you love him and
support him and that you can afford what you have offered and no more.
You are a host, and the guests, even the guests of honor, can't force you
to spend more than you can afford on them. If they press hard, I'm afraid
you'll have to say, without sounding defensive, "I love you. I want to throw
this party for you, but this is what I can offer. Take it or leave it."

FEEDING FRENZY

Hi Elise,

Most of our wedding guests are coming from out of town. My fiancé's parents have offered us a fixed amount for the rehearsal dinner that we can spend as we please.

Given the budget and the guest list, we could serve appetizers for everyone or a sit-down dinner for half the crowd. My mom says we must serve dinner to the wedding party and all out-of-town guests. I disagree. I really love the idea of an intimate rehearsal dinner with just family and close friends. My mom is adamant. What are my options, and how can I convince my mom to go along with me?

—Little Dinner

Dear Little Dinner,

I can't tell you what angles to work with your mother, but demonstrating how much you care about all the out-of-town guests might convince her that you're not being coldhearted. Make a list of restaurants and local amusements to distribute to the guests who might not make the cut. Providing a bit of guidance for the people you won't be seeing may be what she needs to feel comfortable with your decision. If she remains firm in her feelings about including everyone, do consider the cocktails and hors d'oeuvres possibility. It may be worth giving up your desire for intimacy to make her comfortable.

Chapter 12

Ceremony or Talent Show: Vows, Readings, and Performances

When you contemplate wedding ceremonies, do your ears ring with that eternal—if not quite evergreen—march from *Lohengrin*? Do you cringe at the thought of cookie-cutter vows, or squirm at the prospect of sitting through one of those endless talent shows where everyone who isn't a bridesmaid (and a few people who are) gets up to render a song or do a reading? What parts of a wedding are essential, and what can be left on the highway to matrimony for some other happy couple to pick up and take to the altar?

Traditional Basics

- The standard arrangement of family and guests at the ceremony is to have the "bride's side" on the left of the altar and the "groom's side" on the right.
- Getting to the altar: In a traditional church setting (though these protocols can certainly be applied to secular locales as well), the procession starts with the officiant, groom, and best man emerging from the wings of the

church and arranging themselves at the altar. The rest of the wedding party migrates down the aisle, with each group arranged according to height (with the shortest going first) in the following order (either two by two or single file): ushers, bridesmaids, the maid and/or matron of honor, flower girl(s), ring bearer (the children can walk together if it works out well and if the arrangement lessens the chance of them bolting). Finally, the bride enters on her father's right arm. (This is the case even though the bride eventually comes to rest on the groom's left.) It is also in keeping with tradition for the mother of the bride to escort her daughter down the aisle either in addition to or instead of the father, or for the bride to walk alone.

- Once at the altar, the wedding party can be arranged in many ways, though the bride and groom generally stand in front of the altar, with the bride on the groom's left.

- Ceremonies vary widely, depending on religion or lack thereof. As a legal matter, in the United States, the actual language is less important than having a few necessary elements in place:

  ° *A licensed officiant*
  ° *A legal marriage license* (Be aware: Some states have waiting periods between the day the license is issued and the wedding, and of course licenses eventually expire.)
  ° *Witnesses*, if necessary
  ° *Rings:* Most wedding couples have at least a single-ring ceremony (where the groom puts a ring on the ring finger of the bride's left hand), and double-ring ceremonies (where the bride and groom exchange rings) are also popular. Traditionally, the best man is in charge of the ring the groom will give to the bride, and he either keeps it on his person or takes it from

the ring bearer until he gives it to the groom during the ceremony. The maid or matron of honor is, in turn, in charge of the groom's wedding ring. Rings are not necessary for a marriage to be legal.

° *Performances:* Ceremonies are often studded with readings and songs performed by friends and family members. While appealing, these additions are not required, beyond whatever is mandated by religious practices.

° *That kiss:* The bride and groom do not have to kiss at the end of the ceremony. They can, of course, but the decision is entirely up to them. The marriage counts even if they don't go for semipublic displays of affection.

° *Unfamiliar religions:* If guests are invited to a wedding where the ceremony is conducted according to an unfamiliar religion, it is absolutely reasonable for them to ask before the event if there is any protocol they should observe.

° *Recessional:* After the ceremony, the recessional is led by the newlyweds. The wedding party follows. Ushers and bridesmaids can, but do not have to, fall into pairs, particularly if there is an odd number of people on one side. In that case they can be arranged into small rows with the extra people grouped into the middle of the rows. It is best not to leave them trailing at the end of the group, like lost kittens. (Small children who are flower girls or ring bearers do not have to participate in the recessional. They can join their parents in the audience after their trips down the aisle or on their way toward the door.)

° *Throwing things:* It is traditional to throw rice at the newlyweds as they leave the wedding venue, and in recent years, nods to the environment have people launching everything from birdseed to rose petals to butterflies. But there is no need to throw anything at anyone, ever.

° *Receiving lines:* Generally, receiving lines are formed at the reception (see chapter 14, "Sustenance and Civility: The Ins and Outs of the Wedding Reception"), but it is permissible to have them at the wedding venue if the wedding crowd is larger, or if there is not going to be a reception. If people who were not invited to the ceremony will be at the reception, save the receiving line for the reception space. Receiving lines at wedding venues form just outside the location, by the door or on the steps. (For further details about who lines up and in what order, see chapter 14.) There are many advantages to having the receiving line at the reception, not the least of which being that guests will be able to get a drink or a snack while waiting to embrace the newlyweds and their families.

° *Departing:* If cars have been hired to take the wedding party to the reception, the bride and groom leave in one car, the parents of the wedding couple take off in another, the bridesmaids and maid of honor take a third, and the groomsmen pile into a fourth. If there are complicated issues with divorced and remarried parents, these arrangements may need to be reconfigured for everyone's comfort. It is also not necessary to supply cars for everyone. Members of the bridal party (particularly if they have spouses or partners who are wedding guests) may be happier negotiating their own transportation.

Twisting Tradition

One would think that strict etiquette would hold hard and fast to extremely rigid patterns for wedding ceremonies, but even the most traditional authorities relinquish a lot of authority to the scads of religions, all of which have different rules and preferences, all of which are rigid and flexible in different ways, and only a very small number of elements are required for a marriage to be *legal* as far as the government is concerned.

The fact that ceremonies can be so variable does not, however, erase a wide array of uncomfortable situations, most of which stem from the belief that something is *necessary*.

No One Gives Me Away

It doesn't shatter tradition to skip the march down the aisle, let alone walking the walk with your father and having him "give you away" to the groom. If it bothers you, don't do it. The bigger issue is how to deal with a father who wants you on his arm and feels entitled to give you away, if you feel that, well, he shouldn't have much to say about it.

If it helps to point out there is a lot of flexibility in even the most traditional of traditions, tell him. This is particularly effective for brides who have been married before or those who have been living independent lives for a number of years. (Classical etiquette texts usually refer to these women as "older brides." How lovely.) It is also reasonable to be honest and simply say that you feel that getting married was your decision, and you want to be independent as you approach married life.

If there is no way to avoid offending your father, and you still can't bear to have him give you away, you could have both of your parents walk you to the altar (this is the norm in several cultural traditions, and many people who want to honor both parents opt for it anyway). This cuts down a bit on the patriarchal element that might be rubbing you the wrong way and ensures that your mother won't feel left out.

It Isn't a Talent Show

While it is generous to give many people the opportunity to take part in one's wedding ceremony by having them perform readings or songs, keep in mind that the audience of guests, while captive, will get impatient. Choose your performances carefully. Keep them brief and significant.

One pitfall that brides and grooms with small wedding parties face is assigning too many reading slots to people who didn't make the cut as bridesmaids or ushers. This gesture, while sweet, doesn't always sit well. People get offended at being thrown a second-best job. To preserve feelings, make sure that you aren't just bloating the wedding ceremony with wedding-party also-rans, and make sure your friends know how important the reading or song is to the ceremony.

If your friend can't sing, even if he or she thinks otherwise, do not encourage a performance. It will make everyone unhappy. Likewise, if your friend has picked a song or a reading that you do not care for, it is best to reject it while offering some alternative choices. Just don't be the person who keeps nixing all suggestions. That is annoying.

Conversely, if you have been asked to read or perform something that makes you uncomfortable, arm yourself with some alternates of equal or shorter length. You may not win the debate, and if you don't, just remember that this isn't your wedding. If it makes your friend happy to have you read or sing something stupid, understand that no one will really be watching you, anyway. The only way you can call negative attention to yourself is by intentionally performing badly or acting like a sourpuss.

You Can Leave God Out

All the classic wedding vows mention God. If you are agnostic or atheist or just prefer a purely secular ceremony, you can ask to leave God out. This is, of course, more difficult if your officiant is affiliated with any particular religion, or if your officiant performs dozens of ceremonies a week and is prone to using God-focused language reflexively, as part of a standard ceremony (as happens in popular elopement spots such as Las Vegas), so be vigilant and clear about what you want or do not want in your vows.

Multiple Religions?

Weddings merge families, so it shouldn't be surprising that they often call for a merging of religious backgrounds as well. This can happen harmoniously and it can also involve some discomfort, since belief and spirituality are often private matters, dearly and closely held. Parents can suddenly feel very strongly about religion, when prior to any wedding chatter, they couldn't have seemed less interested; brides or grooms who have lived relatively agnostic lives may want to marry at the familiar church they went to as children. If a new religion has been embraced, this may be the chance to show it off; and if the bride and groom come from wildly different backgrounds, negotiations are in order. Bottom line: It is likely that everyone is going to have to bend at least a little bit.

The best, though never foolproof, plan to navigate weddings with more than one religious influence is to start planning the ceremony early and discuss issues regularly with all the people most inclined to whine or act betrayed. It may seem easier to keep everything on the Q.T., but opting to have ceremony surprises when you know your family will flip is just encouraging a *Casablanca* moment (i.e., something you will regret, "maybe not today, maybe not tomorrow, but soon and for the rest of your life").

Different plans work for different religions, so a certain amount of flexibility is in order. The greatest compromise will need to happen for people whose religions require both bride and groom to be on the same spiritual path and mandate that someone has to convert. In situations where conversion is not an acceptable compromise, the wedding couple may have to choose to marry in a less rigid religious environment. For some, dual ceremonies work well, with officiants from each religion performing part of the wedding. Generally, only one of the officiants will handle the legal paperwork in these situations. In other cases, it may be easier to have two entirely separate weddings—each under the auspices of a different religion. This plan can be more expensive, but it can also satisfy family members who are nervous about dual ceremonies. The two-ceremony plan also works well for couples in which one party is agnostic or atheist. Having a legal courthouse wedding one day and a religious ceremony on another occasion can acknowledge both sets of beliefs—or their absence.

Destination Ceremonies

If you are getting married abroad, it is important to embrace your inner librarian and figure out as soon as possible what you need to do to make your marriage legal. Every country has different rules, some of which may interfere with your plans. The solution to this problem is to have a civil ceremony at home to get the legal issues out of the way and open the field for a foreign ceremony without impediments. There is nothing rude about doing this.

Unofficial Officiants

What if you want your novelist friend or yoga instructor or father or Interesting Neighbor to perform your wedding ceremony, but your choice officiant has no official credentials? You could encourage your would-be master of ceremonies to become legally certified in your state, but it is also just as easy to, again, trot over to city hall, get hitched in the eyes of the law, and then have your real ceremony, during which your friend marries you in a way that satisfies you personally.

Etiquette in Action

HONORS FOR NONBRIDESMAIDS

Dear Elise,

My fiancé and I are only having a best man and a matron of honor. I have two close friends who really wanted to plan a shower and a bachelorette party. I am happy that they are so excited, but I do not want them to be disappointed about not being bridesmaids. Are there other "VIP" roles they can play in the wedding?

　　—Grateful

Dear Grateful,

Wonderful friends, no strife—how lucky can you get? Ask around and you'll hear tales of weddings littered with the corpses of friendships, broken on the rocky shores of Bridesmaidland. In choosing not to have bridesmaids, you may have taken the best route to happiness. Don't feel guilty for not giving them additional responsibilities or expenses.

　　As far as honors go, you could certainly have your friends do readings in the ceremony, but you could also thank them publicly, with a nice big toast. While the most notorious toasts are given by fathers of brides and by best men, there is nothing keeping you from simply jumping up, glass in hand, and saluting your friends.

INVITING A GHOST

Dear Elise,

My fiancé met me shortly after his wife passed away. He really wants to mention his first marriage in our wedding ceremony.

I really don't want her name to be part of our wedding. If his first wife is talked about in the ceremony, I think the guests would wonder whether my fiancé is really over her. I am truly really sorry for his loss, but I think our wedding should be about us. I feel sick over this.

—Ceremony Issues

Dear Ceremony Issues,

Of course you feel compromised. Your future husband has invited a ghost to your wedding. Including a discussion of his first wife in your ceremony is completely awkward, since it entails inserting a former lover into the text of your marriage. While you can happily acknowledge his first wife's presence in his consciousness in private, there is no need for her to take a place of significance in your vows. There should be other ways for him to assuage his feelings of guilt.

Rather than draw a line in the sand, talk to your fiancé about some kind of compromise. Let him know what is and is not comfortable for you. Most people who marry for a second time don't feel obliged to mention the previous marriage in the wedding ceremony itself. But if you truly have no problem with this, you can say that you won't mind having your officiant mention your fiancé's previous happy marriage in passing, but you do not want your ceremony to be haunted by a discussion of his first wife or even a mention of her name.

If you want to offer your fiancé an opportunity to acknowledge his first wife, suggest that he give a toast at the reception about his first marriage, which gave him his wonderful past, and how excited he is that you have joined his family and extended his good fortune. That way he is acknowledging her while giving you credit for the life you have together.

Clearly your fiancé has quite a bit of unresolved guilt, but he should deal with it privately. Including his first wife in the ceremony will only complicate a delicate situation. Marriage vows are not meant to be biographies. They are contracts administered by an officiant and witnessed by people who love the bride and groom.

TWO FATHERS: HOW TO PROCEED

Dear Elise,

I am twice divorced. My son is getting married, and when the wedding party is introduced in the reception hall, the parents will be introduced. I will be there, along with his natural father and his stepfather who raised him. My son does not want to hurt either of these men, and he does not want to give higher billing to either one of them, so he is thinking of having me come out with the bride's parents and not having them introduced at all. What else can we do?

—Mother of the Groom

Dear Mother of the Groom,

Your son has plenty of choices, and a lot depends on how well everyone gets along. Are you averse to walking between your two former husbands? You wouldn't have to have extensive contact with them. Alternatively, you could enter first and your former husbands could follow you.

Your son could exclude both his natural father and his stepfather, and this decision would be "safe" as far as treating everyone equally, but really, does he gain anything with this gesture? The point of the reception introduction is to give the bride and groom and their families a moment in the sun, so your son ostentatiously omitting his biological father and stepfather might suggest some sort of rift in their relationship.

There is no strict policy for how you handle these choices, but the key is realizing that this is all about appearances—it is a procession into the reception, after all.

NO ESCORT, PLEASE

Dear Elise,

I've never been close to my father, but now I feel like I'm caught in the Twilight Zone because he and his second wife want to contribute to my wedding. I want to be independent and walk down the aisle alone, but my father wants to escort me. I don't know if I can have him walk with me without feeling bullied. Is there a way to be a polite, grateful daughter while standing up for myself?

—Wants to Be Grown-Up

Dear Wants,

Weddings do strange things to the human psyche. They possess people and make them suddenly want to embrace tradition, even if the corresponding emotion is absent. They make people see the symbolism in gestures that ordinarily don't bear much more than a second thought. There is no easy way to break the Wedding Spell, I'm afraid. It is far more powerful than common sense.

This doesn't mean you must bend to your father's wishes, but decide how strongly you feel about this. If not wanting help down the aisle is nonnegotiable, you're entitled to stick to your guns. You just may want to compromise elsewhere.

You don't mention the details of your wedding, but if you aren't having a wedding party, you could weasel your way around the issue by forgoing a procession entirely. Or you could sit down with your father, talk to him about your squeamishness, and offer him an alternative: Perhaps you wouldn't mind if he had a father/daughter dance with you, or maybe there is some other gesture he would like to make (a toast, maybe). Would you be open to him escorting someone else (such as your mother or his wife) down the aisle as part of your procession? There are a number of possibilities, and I think you can be honest with him about how this one tradition makes you feel without implying that you are rejecting him.

HOW TO INTRODUCE

Dear Elise,

I'm not taking my fiancé's last name, and the officiant asked how we want to be announced as man and wife after the ring exchange. I don't want him to say "Mr. and Mrs. X," since I won't *be* "Mrs." What do people usually do in this situation?

—Same-Name Bride

Dear Same-Name,

You can do whatever you'd like as far as announcements go. You can even skip the announcement entirely. If you choose to go with the introduction, think about how you'd like to present yourself. There is nothing wrong with your officiant saying, "Allow me to introduce the newlyweds: Bride's Name and Groom's Name."

Remember, this is a formality, not a necessity, so if you want to make the announcement, think about the two pieces of information you want to convey: (1) You are married, and (2) you are keeping your name. Once you determine the essence of the message, you can write any kind of short declaration you like.

Chapter 13

Gathering the Nearest and Dearest:
Guest Behavior

Sure, it all *seems* so obvious when the crisp, cream-colored envelope with the pastel stamp shows up in the mailbox. But then you start to study the contents, and suddenly the mind begins to reel with questions. What looked simple enough is now a headache-inducing brainteaser, and you're tempted to shove that elegantly designed creation to the bottom of the mail heap.

Don't do it. It isn't hard to face the music. All you need to know are the basic ground rules and a sense of what to do if your hosts' behavior strays from the norm.

Traditional Basics

Because wedding invitations are so extremely codified, it is often assumed that prospective guests know what's expected of them, not only in terms of responding promptly and not showing up with a raft of extra guests, but also when it comes to general nuptial conduct. The unwritten policies are pretty straightforward, but only if you already know what they are. For the uninitiated, here's a crash course.

- Prospective guests should respond to wedding invitations as soon as possible. This keeps the wedding couple from having to hound them. (If people fail to RSVP, the wedding couple, or the wedding hosts, are going to have to call or write to them at the eleventh hour to inquire about their plans. It is reasonable to do this, but hosts find it incredibly annoying, at a moment when time is short.)

- If invitees are offered the option to bring a "guest," they should indicate the name of their date on the response card, so that their hosts know who is attending and can assign seats at the reception.

- Guests should not assume that their children have been invited to the wedding unless the kids' names or the words "and Family" are written on the inner envelope that contains the invitation. (Actually, "and Family" is meant to include all family members living at one residence—including grandparents, uncles, great-aunts, you name it—and grown children living out of the house should get their own invitations sent to them.) If both the inner and outer envelopes are addressed to only one person, then only that person is being invited—no date, no kid, no nothing.

- Clothing: Guests should gauge their attire according to the time and place of the wedding and respond to any hints offered by the wedding hosts. Some houses of worship have dress protocols (that women's arms be covered and not much décolletage be revealed, for instance). Evening dress should not be worn before six o'clock p.m. Only members of the wedding party should wear live flowers.

- Guests should expect to finance their transportation to the wedding and their own accommodations. It is reasonable for guests to ask their hosts for suggestions regarding local hotels if none were provided.

- No one should show up late for the wedding ceremony.

- In weddings with ushers, guests will be asked, upon entering, if they are from the bride's side or the groom's side. Depending on the answer, they will be seated on the left or the right side of the aisle. The usher will take a woman by the arm and guide her to a spot. With couples, the usher will either take the woman's arm, leaving her companion to trail just behind them, or he will let the couple walk together just behind him. Female couples or teams of women who arrive together are treated the same way (either one on an arm and one behind, or both walk behind the usher), and male couples walk behind the usher.

- If guests are unfamiliar with the religion in which the ceremony is being conducted, they should simply observe and be guided by the people around them when it comes to simple gestures (such as standing or sitting). No one would want guests to do anything that compromised their beliefs, so if guests feel uncomfortable doing anything, they should not be pressured into participating against their inclinations, though they should not make a big deal about abstaining.

- Unless guests are told otherwise, they are responsible for their own transportation from the wedding venue to the reception.

- At the reception, guests should go through the receiving line as soon as possible to get it over with. Generally, the bride's mother is the first person on the receiving line to greet guests. Guests should be jolly and briefly introduce themselves and their dates (if they're not already acquainted with the wedding party). This is also the moment when guests who are giving cash presents or checks can hand them to the bride and groom. This is not the time to get involved in long conversations—quick handshakes and kisses and best wishes are safest. Guests should not say "congratulations" to the bride. It is considered unlucky. Why? As is the case with so many wedding superstitions, the policy of congratulating only the groom and offering one's best wishes to the bride has murky origins. Traditional etiquette texts are adamant about the rule but rarely explain that it derives from an obscure, probably Victorian, sense of courtesy. To say "congratulations" to the bride is to suggest that she either went out of her way to pursue and trap her new husband into marrying her, or that she is especially fortunate to be marrying at all. It is much more gallant to congratulate the groom, implying that, of the two, he is the lucky one. Somehow this gentle courtesy turned into a full-blown taboo.

- Dancing: Guests wait to dance at least until after the bride and groom have their first dance together. (See chapter 14, "Sustenance and Civility: The Ins and Outs of the Wedding Reception," for the formal list of dances that happen before guests are free to join in.)

- Toasts: Unless guests have been invited to propose a toast, they should refrain from giving one.

- Single female guests may want to participate in the bouquet toss, which generally happens toward the end of the reception. Sometimes, only bridesmaids are allowed to be bouquet catchers. (This is a very traditional way to handle the bouquet toss, and it is becoming less and less popular.) If this is the case, guests shouldn't be miffed, but if they are included in this tradition, they should hop into the fray and watch for flying elbows.

- Guests can leave wedding receptions at any point. A good "early" moment to make a break for it is just after the cake is cut. It is nice to thank the bride and groom before hitting the road, but if they are unavailable, guests should track down the bride's or groom's parents and let them know how much they enjoyed themselves.

- Presents: Unless it has been otherwise specified before the wedding, presents are generally sent to the bride at home (or to the bride and groom if they live together). After the wedding, gifts are sent to the newlyweds at home. Bringing presents to the wedding and reception can be tricky. The wedding couple, tired and possibly soused, will have to figure out how to transport everything out of the reception venue, and often they will be stuck shipping everything home. (This is especially true for destination weddings.) It is safest to send gifts before or after the fact.

Twisting Tradition

Why all the hullabaloo? Aren't weddings just parties, only bigger and dressier than usual? Well, they *are*, but how often do you party with your friends' distant relatives? It doesn't undermine anyone's fun to keep in mind that weddings are significant events—for the newlyweds, if not for everyone (or even *anyone*) else. Modern guests often misplace standard courtesies in this era of happy informality. Here are some areas in which a casual approach to someone else's wedding can be truly unpleasant.

There's Nothing Wrong with Being Invited

Occasionally people receive wedding invitations from friends who have drifted away or extremely distant relatives, and since it is customary always to think the worst of everyone, they assume that the invitation is part of some nefarious agenda—a "gift grab" or "social climb."

Give everyone a break. The wedding couple may like you. Their parents may have wanted to invite you. The couple may be inviting other relatives to whom they are just as distantly related but with whom they are emotionally close, and they correctly wanted to be consistent with their invitations. An invitation is only a nice thing. (Even the language should tell you that—how often is your potential presence described as an "honor" or a "pleasure"?) It isn't a jail sentence. If you don't want to go, don't. Send in your regrets and sit it out. You don't even need to send a present, so put the whole "greedy bride" concept out of your mind.

Don't Wheedle for an Invite

There are many reasons for exclusive guest lists. If you weren't invited to a wedding, don't try to force yourself on the wedding couple or demand to be there. That only makes you look unstable and doesn't help your cause. If being excluded from the guest list is speaking loudly to you about the state of your friendship, that is something to address with your friends separately, but using guilt or begging or tantrum throwing to secure what you want is never a good idea.

Make Up Your Mind

There's the invitation, complete with response card and stamp so you don't have to steal one from the office manager or brave the post office. What are you going to do about it?

Check your calendar, make up your mind, fill out the card, and send it back. That is it.

Of course, there can be mitigating circumstances. There can also be issues about whether you can bring your new boyfriend, who wasn't in the picture when your friend finished sweating over the guest list. It is not beyond the pale to ask if you could attend accompanied by your new paramour, but remember that your friend might not be able to accommodate extra people. (Keep in mind that the decision might be greater than just allowing *your* extra person. It may be that if your friends allow you to bring a date, they would have to open the floodgates, and they are unable to afford all the additional people.) If that is the case, don't sulk, just decide whether or not you can attend and be gracious about it.

Don't Be a No-Show

Sure you were going to go; your outfit is even ready for pickup at the dry cleaners, but something came up—you got sick, your dog needs surgery, your ceiling fell in, work couldn't spring you . . . there are many reasons, all of which are pressing to you and few of which will resonate with much depth to your friends in the throes of wedding planning. You don't have to explain elaborately why you won't be able to attend, but you do need to say something, and you need to speak up as soon as possible. The rudeness of silence comes from your hosts feeling you just didn't care enough about them or their event (for which they're surely spending a lot of money) to let them know your change of plans. They, in turn, should not be critical of your reasons for backing out. But treating a wedding as if it were some drop-in keg party where you don't have to bother saying what your plans are one way or the other, or even show up, is guaranteed to hurt feelings.

What About the Children?

It will be obvious from the invitation you receive whether the pleasure of your kids' company is requested or not. If they are not named on the envelope, they are not invited. Do not take this personally. It is unlikely that the bride and groom have decided they like all kids except yours. The decision to exclude children is generally universal and involves questions of taste (what sort of wedding the bride and groom want to have) and practicality (depending on how many children are in question, it could cost a lot to feed and entertain all of them, and if the event is late at night, it may be hard to keep them happy and awake).

Understandably, not being able to bring your children to a wedding can make things complicated. You need to find a babysitter, which means you may have to shell out more money than you would like, or it means—in the case of weddings that require travel or actual destination weddings—that you'll have to make a lot of decisions. Will you leave your child or children at home with known caregivers? Will you make it a family trip and use a local sitter? Will you go at all?

Whatever you decide to do is fair, but don't seize the opportunity to tell your prospective hosts what a hardship attending their wedding will be for you or how much you would have loved to attend the nuptials, but you can't bear to spend any time away from your child. Make your plans and RSVP accordingly.

If you have an extenuating circumstance in the form of a nursing infant, for instance, you are free to ask your hosts if the no-children rule applies to children who can't even sit up on their own. The bride and groom may make exceptions for newborns, but if they don't, you're again faced with having to make a choice.

Remember, if this wedding is a no-kids affair, yours are not the only ones being excluded. It isn't personal, and while it may feel like a rejection, try to think about the big picture.

When It's a "Working Wedding" for Your Partner

He's a member of the wedding party and you aren't. It happens, and while you're just as glad that you didn't have to shell out for a bridesmaid dress for someone you don't really know, it's a little difficult having your companion constantly whisked away for photo ops and groomsman duties.

Take this into account before you make plans to attend the wedding. Will you be happy enough spending some time on your own? If it will truly infuriate you, it might be best to stay home. On the other hand, if you attend, you could have the best of both worlds—a chance to meet new people and have some independence while not flying completely solo.

When Your Seat Doesn't Satisfy

At the reception, if your partner is seated at a different table, or at a different part of the table from you, do not get snitty and start rearranging place cards. That is beyond naughty. A lot of sweat and tears got poured into that seating plan. Sit tight. You'll be fine eating one meal in the company of strangers, and take the opportunity to mill around. No one stays put for the whole reception.

When You Hate One of the Newlyweds

It's as inevitable as the freshman fifteen: At some point in your life, a good friend is going to marry someone awful. At the wedding, you will be expected to be jolly and say happy things. White lies won't hurt anyone, but what if those words just lodge in your throat, refusing to emerge? Keep these phrases handy:

- When cornered by your friend: "I'm so happy for you."
- When quizzed by someone you don't know about the new bride or groom: "I don't know [him/her] very well but [he/she] seems to make [Sandra/ Harold] very happy."
- Generic air filler: "They do look great together."

Bad Kids

If children are misbehaving in a way that is dangerous to themselves, to any person, or to the venue, it is not rude to tell their parents. If they are merely insufferably annoying, do not speak to their parents about their behavior. Find another drink and be glad the little monsters aren't your responsibility.

Bad Drunks

The obnoxious, stupid drunk is a wedding cliché, and one that is generally not particularly welcome.

If you are prone to quaffing heavily, consider this: You don't want to be the person responsible for creating all sorts of unpleasant memories and pictures. You're a guest, and often that means you can drink as much as you like, but it also means you should behave with a degree of dignity and respect. You can always get just drunk enough to be happy and then finish off the job by drinking excessively once you get home or back to the hotel, or find a local bar after the reception.

If you're faced with a friend or relative who is prone to overindulging so much that he or she is guaranteed to make a fool of him- or herself, there are a couple of discreet routes to take. You can always solicit the help of a couple of other relatives or friends to be gentle "minders," who can steer the lush away from the bar with conversation and dancing. Another option is to make the waitstaff and bartenders aware of the problem drinkers and instruct them to cut off the guest in question if he or she gets too sloshed. (For more information on drinking at the reception, see chapter 14, "Sustenance and Civility: The Ins and Outs of the Wedding Reception.")

======== *Etiquette in Action* ========

HUNTING GUESTS

Dear Elise,

The RSVPs for my wedding are due. How do I handle people who have not responded? What does one say? Should my fiancé call his friends and relatives and I call mine? What if I can't reach people? Could I send e-mails? If they still don't reply, should I assume that they are attending? How many times should I try to reach someone?

—Just Want to Know the Number

Dear Just Want to Know,

You aren't alone. Very few people who throw formal parties of any kind escape having to track down some guests to find out whether or not they're attending. Before you get too angry, embark on a calling spree and see if you can't pin people down.

There's no reason you should have to do this alone, so chop your list of delinquent potential guests in half and get your fiancé to join the telephone marathon. When you call, just say that you sent your friend/relative a wedding invitation and haven't heard back, and you need to know if the friend/relative will be attending. You can give a date by which you need a final head count as a deadline, and say that if you haven't heard you will assume they are not coming, if that makes you more comfortable. If e-mail works better for some people, you can certainly write to them, since there is no strict procedure. For your own sake, don't sound impatient or angry. You're still hoping people will come, and nothing makes a party sound less appealing than an angry host or hostess (even if the guests are completely remiss).

<hr>

MARITAL STATE AND HOTEL ROOM

Dear Elise,

A relative is getting married, and she reserved a block of hotel rooms for guests. My boyfriend and I reserved a room, but my mother told me that this is a family affair and we could not share a room because this would insult the bride's family. For the record, my partner and I have been together for years, and I know the bride and groom don't care at all if we bunk up. Would it really be a faux pas to stay in a hotel room together just because the bride's parents might notice?

—One Room

Dear One Room,

You aren't staying in your relatives' private bed-and-breakfast, where they will bound into your room at some ungodly hour with waffles and muffins and be shocked to see you and your boyfriend together, are you? You aren't expecting your relative's parents to pick up your hotel tab, are you?

If you answered no to both these questions, then you can reasonably expect to be treated the way other guests are treated: with a degree of privacy. If your relatives have nothing better to think about on the eve of their daughter's wedding than whether a committed unmarried couple is sleeping in the same room, they deserve to be shocked or disappointed. Why would they care what you do, anyway?

In a nutshell: It is not their business whether you and your partner sleep in the same or different rooms during this wedding weekend.

Does your mother have some sort of issue with unmarried couples sharing hotel rooms during wedding weekends? Is she trying to fob off her discomfort on her relatives? It doesn't matter in practice, since you are well within your rights to stick to your one room that will allow you to save some money and probably have a better time. From now on, just don't mention your arrangement to your mother. If she asks, tell her that you are taking responsibility for your accommodations and she doesn't have to worry about it. Unless you feel the potential for a rift is so great that shelling out for another room is a wise tactical move, you don't have to do anything you don't want to do.

Your relatives should not be concerned about your sleeping arrangements, and if they ask or tell your mother to ask about them, try the reply, "Why are you interested?" This should not be a battle, so your best bet is not to rise to any provocation.

MISGUIDED GROOMSPERSON

Dear Elise,

My fiancé has a woman in his wedding party who doesn't like me. I don't think I should have to deal with her nastiness at my wedding.

My fiancé said he would ask her to bow out if her unpleasant behavior toward me continues, but that would probably end their friendship. Is it wrong of me to let him fire her? He talked to her, and she said she would improve, but so far she hasn't.

—What's with Her?

Dear What's With,

There are two mysteries here, neither of which has anything to do with you. First, why did your fiancé decide this woman was a good choice to stand up with him at his wedding? And second, why did this woman think it would be a good idea for her to have to honor a situation she clearly can't handle?

These questions raise issues that point to etiquette violations. One shouldn't ask someone to be in one's wedding if that person will suffer from merely witnessing the nuptials; and if one is inclined to be melodramatic, abusive, and awful at having to stand up for a certain wedding, one should beg off. That is the beginning and end of it.

If this woman's behavior has not let up, you are well within your rights to ask your fiancé if he wants this situation to continue. It is obvious his friend is being made unhappy, and you should point out that she would not only be *his* groomsperson, but she would be standing up as part of the larger wedding party, supposedly supporting him in his union. If she can't do that, she really shouldn't be participating in the wedding, and instead she can just be a sullen guest. Every wedding has one anyway, and she's got a head start on the sulks.

Your fiancé should be able to recognize that this situation is desperately unhappy and should take control of the matter. If he doesn't see what's going on, ask him if he really wants someone as angry, nasty, and unsupportive standing up with him. Leave the decision up to him as to whether he fires her or has another heart-to-heart with her. Don't force the issue, but prepare a few choice things to say when she is unpleasant. Would you like a few? Here:

—"Why would you say that?"

—"I'm sorry you feel that way, but I'm not canceling my wedding."

—"Would you like some more cake?"

Don't get angry; just let her see that she isn't doing herself any favors.

CARDED AT A WEDDING

Dear Elise,

I just went to a wedding at a hotel. This was the first wedding I've been to since turning twenty-one, and I wanted a celebratory drink, but I didn't bring ID, since I wasn't driving—I'd come with my parents. The bartender carded at the open bar, the waiter carded when we got to the table. A waiter even scolded my mother for giving me a sip of her wine! I thought weddings were exempt from underage drinking laws because they are private celebrations and don't sell drinks. Did the waiters have to be so rude?

—Never Forgetting My ID Again

Dear Never Forgetting,

The short answer is that, while laws can vary from state to state, no establishment should provide minors with alcoholic beverages, whether the minors are paying for them or not, and the hotel was doing what it had to do to protect itself. Hotels and restaurants can lose their liquor licenses by serving minors. This is no sudden "crackdown." The laws have been in place in most of the United States for some time and generally apply to establishments that have liquor licenses and serve alcohol, no matter who pays.

As for the relative civility of the waitstaff, it is true that the waiters should not have gotten nasty, but I suspect these folks were getting a certain amount of flak from all the folks who showed up sans ID. Perhaps they had reached their limit of arguing. Remember, in this circumstance, they would have been the ones to get in trouble for your drinking had you been underage, not you or your parents. If they were to let you drink, they would be putting their jobs and the establishment at risk. In the future, always take your ID.

BUT I DO HAVE A DATE

Dear Elise,

My nephew is getting married. The wedding is quite large. I am single. My brother's wife, her siblings, and their spouses are also invited. I was the only person in the groom's immediate family who was not invited with a guest. I would like to bring someone. Also, the rest of the family was invited to the engagement party. I was not invited because they figured I wouldn't come because I don't live nearby (I was never consulted).

Do I have the right to be upset, and, since it looks like etiquette was not followed, can I continue to ignore protocol and handwrite "and Guest" on the invite?

—Feeling Insulted

Dear Feeling,

It is almost never a good idea to respond to rudeness with more rudeness. The initial offenders won't learn their lessons, and they'll only use your transgression (however justified) as ammunition against you.

You should not just write "and Guest" on your invitation and expect it to be well received. There is a different, less passive-aggressive approach to take. Call your sibling or your nephew and explain your situation. Put it to them bluntly but nicely. They may have made an honest mistake. You can also tell them that you would have been happy to attend the engagement party and get everything out in the open. Your hurt feelings demonstrate why hosts should let their prospective guests decide if they want to be inconvenienced enough to attend a party and not try to be mind readers.

The whole "and Guest" construct is uncomfortable for many people, and traditionally, there is only a mandate to invite people with significant others who can be named on an invitation. Having said this, even if they are avoiding the "and Guest" format, they certainly could have asked you if you wanted to bring a date.

If you ask nicely if you can bring your friend, and your sibling and nephew deny you, then you have a different problem. If you are really hurt, you can decide not to go to the wedding, but don't bring someone uninvited. Not only will this backfire, but your friend will be made uncomfortable, and you don't need that on top of your own disappointment.

Chapter 14

Sustenance and Civility:
The Ins and Outs of the Wedding Reception

The deed is done! Now everyone can relax, dance, eat, drink, and . . . what else are you supposed to do at the reception? Wedding reception traditions abound. They come from every culture, cater to any whim, and purport to serve many useful purposes. Does everyone have to dance? What if you're a single bridesmaid who doesn't want to take part in the bouquet toss? How early can you make your exit?

Traditional Basics

- *Receiving lines:* Traditionally, the receiving line forms early in the reception, so that introductions can be made and gotten over with. When guests arrive, they drop off their coats, grab a drink, and hop on line to wish everyone the best. The receiving line should form someplace where it doesn't cause a logjam.

  - The wedding participant lineup at the reception is the same as it would be if the receiving line happened at the ceremony location (which is equally acceptable). The mother of the bride stands next to the bride or groom (the bride is always on the groom's right), followed by the maid or matron of honor—or both if there are both—and the bridesmaids (if it is determined that they will be on the line). The fathers of the bride and groom can opt to join the receiving line as well (if they participate, they stand beside their wives). Flower girls and ring bearers are never pressed into this service. Traditionally, divorced parents do not stand in line together. The parent who is hosting should do the honors.

° Guests should introduce themselves and greet the wedding party quickly and shouldn't be too concerned with what they say (though they should avoid the word "congratulations" when speaking with the bride, which is considered bad luck). Very few people remember the exchanges they have on the receiving line unless they are notably offensive.

° It is not necessary to have a receiving line at all, especially if the crowd isn't massive.

- *Guest books:* Couples sometimes like to encourage their guests to sign a book and jot down some words of encouragement. The guest book is usually placed on an easily accessed table near the entrance to the reception. Often a friend or relative is assigned to monitor guest book activity and encourage people to sign it (this can be a good job for children, but it is a drag for most adults).
- *Food:* Receptions can happen over any mealtime (breakfast, lunch, dinner) or in between (cocktails, tea, dessert), at many levels of formality, though wedding "breakfasts" often have a lunch-type menu. Meals can be buffet-style or served by a waitstaff.
- *Seating:* There are a few standard seating arrangements. Traditionally, there can be assigned seating for all the guests, or assigned seating can be reserved for the bride and groom, their families, and the wedding party, while the

rest of the guests fend for themselves. Either is perfectly proper. Assigned seats are not mandatory for anyone, though they can be very convenient.

° The key tables are often the Bride's Table and the Parents' Table. The Bride's Table seats the bride (on the groom's right, as always) with the best man beside her, the maid of honor on the groom's left, and the rest of the wedding party, alternating male/female, filling out the table. The Parents' Table has the groom's mother sitting to the right of the bride's father and the groom's father sitting to the right of the bride's mother. The rest of the table is filled with grandparents, godparents, other close relatives, and the officiant and his or her spouse (if they have been invited, which they generally are). Divorced parents should not sit at the same table.

• *Toasts:* The traditional toasting beverage is champagne, but substitutions can be made. The first toast usually is given by the best man, whose words should be brief, a little corny, amusing, and not embarrassing. When he is done, everyone except the bride and groom raises a glass and drinks the toast. The groom then stands, thanks everyone, and toasts his new wife. Alternatively, the wedding's hosts can give the first toast, welcoming everyone. It used to be common for people who were unable to travel to the wedding to send telegrams or letters to be read at the reception. If you have them, this is the moment to read them (and it is up to the bride and groom to decide who will read these missives). No other toasts are required, though the bride and groom may invite others to step up. Often this is something they plan ahead of time in an effort to ward off toast-happy relatives and friends who enjoy going on and on. The best way to end toasts is to start dancing or cut the cake.

- *Cake:* The most traditional wedding cake is something few embrace: fruit-cake. (It certainly lasts forever, which says a lot for its symbolism if not for its flavor.) But even if one forgoes fruitcake, there are some other cake traditions they can employ. If the reception is a sit-down dinner, it is standard to cut the cake just before dessert is served, which permits guests to have double dessert (cake *and* anything else). The traditional protocol is for the bride and groom together to cut the first slice of cake from the bottom tier. They then have the choice of feeding bites of cake to each other or not. It is *not* standard practice for the groom to smash cake in his bride's face, so only do it if you want to. The cake is then taken to the kitchen to slice up.

  ° The top (smallest) tier of the cake is wrapped up for the bride and groom to take home, freeze, and attempt to enjoy on their first anniversary.

- *Dancing:* As with so much wedding tradition, the protocol lies mostly in the order of things, rather than specifics (the dances can be to any song, for instance).

  ° *Standard dance order:* The bride and groom have the first dance together. Then the father of the groom dances with the bride. The father of the bride cuts in after a while and dances with his daughter. (If they would prefer, the bride and her father could dance to a separate song instead of having him cut in.) In the meantime, the groom dances with the bride's mother and then with his own. For the third dance, the bride's father dances with the groom's mother and the groom's father dances with the bride's mother, while the groom dances with the maid of honor, the bride dances with the best man, and the ushers dance with the bridesmaids. At this point it is fair for the guests to get up and start dancing. Yet another tradition holds that—within reason—all male guests should try to snag a fragment of a dance with the bride.

°   The above may be too complicated for any number of reasons, including divorced parents or the absence of a wedding party, in which case general dancing can commence after the bride and groom have their first dance together.

- *Wrapping up the reception:* A few traditions signal the end of the party.

°   *Bouquet toss:* The bride collects her single bridesmaids and (if she isn't following the ancient bridesmaids-only tradition) gathers the single female guests (and male guests if they want to join in) and has them gather at the foot of a staircase or in some other convenient bouquet-catching spot. She then ascends the stairs (or walks away to achieve some tossing distance), turns her back (to ensure impartiality), and throws her bouquet into the crowd. *Bouquet alternative*: Sometimes the bride's bouquet is sent to a friend or relative who is unable to attend the wedding. This can be a good way to dodge the tossing tradition, though if you want to keep the tossing *and* give the bouquet away, you can always have a second bouquet on hand.

°   *Garter toss:* Notably, there is little discussion of the infamous garter toss in the annals of traditional etiquette. (It is similar to the bouquet toss, except it involves the groom removing a garter from his bride's leg and throwing it to a crowd of men.) Unless everyone feels a compelling reason to embrace this semihumiliating convention, it should be skipped, and the bride and groom really shouldn't be bullied into something they don't want to do. There is some tradition for the bouquet catcher and the garter catcher to have a dance together.

- *When to hit the road:* Traditionalists believe that the bride and groom should make their exit before the bulk of their guests get tired and only linger because they feel they must. This is not, strictly speaking, a necessary courtesy, since guests really are allowed to go at any time.
- *Bride and groom depart:* Standard protocol has the bride—with the assistance of her mother and maid or matron of honor (and possibly bridesmaids)— changing into her "traveling dress." She then says good-bye to her new husband's parents.
- *Leaving:* As the bride and groom make their exit, all the remaining guests throw rose petals, confetti, rice, etc., on them for luck. (This practice is often roundly discouraged by venues, so it is a tradition that may have to be forgone for contractual reasons.)

Twisting Tradition

Reception protocol is actually rather spare, and a lot of times people are faced with "presumed tradition" rather than anything that is actually required. Many rituals, if they seem overwhelming or annoying, can be jettisoned or curtailed without ill effect. The opposite is also true: Invoking certain traditions or occasionally being a bit rigid can make everyone more comfortable.

Picky Eaters

If it isn't a diet, it's an allergy. If it isn't an allergy, it's a "sensitivity." If it isn't an allergy or sensitivity, it's a religious or philosophical restriction, or a simple preference disguised as a diet, allergy, sensitivity, or religio-philosophical restriction. Two basic points must be understood. First, the hosts are not responsible for the extremes of guest diets or food fussiness, though they should make an effort to meet everyone halfway with some broad gestures (for instance, coming up with a vegetarian alternative or warning people who are severely allergic to mushrooms that tasty fungi will make an appearance in the ravioli). Second, guests are responsible for dealing with their own extensive dietary peculiarities (if they are strict vegans, they should arm themselves with some "safe" snacks, just in case all vegetables get a butter shower), and they should not go into the affair believing that this should be the best meal they will ever have, full of all their favorite treats. If they want such a bonanza, they can plan their own reception.

Standard reception food tends to be rather conservative (roast chicken, grilled steak, poached salmon with dill sauce), but there is no reason to embrace the bland—especially if you're concerned about having to feed a crowd of many tastes. Italian food, for example, can offer many vegetarian options that aren't so aggressively vegetarian as to freak out the carnivores in the crowd (pasta dishes are familiar to everyone, while tofu still has residual "weird" connotations to some).

The Shellfish Conundrum

It is a wedding myth that you must serve shrimp cocktail in order to avoid seeming cheap. As long as you serve tasty food, you don't need to offer a most succulent (if expensive) crustacean, and prawns represent a truly ridiculous reason to bankrupt yourself.

Everyone Eats

Something that often gets forgotten in the rush of wedding planning is that it is absolutely necessary to feed the wedding vendors. Band members, DJs, event planners, photographers, videographers, day-of planners . . . the whole lot must be nourished. Everyone is working hard to make your wedding great, and they expect and deserve this courtesy. It is remarkable how many wedding couples pursuing "high-class" weddings think it is somehow gauche to feed the people who are working for them, when it is infinitely more unrefined to treat vendors like slaves.

So arrange for your staff to have meals available (caterers can easily budget for this) and talk to them about how and when they would like to eat them. Since photographers, for instance, are often documenting the reception, it might be easier for them to have their food available at another time.

The Perils of Drink

There is absolutely nothing wrong with serving alcohol in any of its many legal forms at wedding receptions. It becomes a problem only when people get wishy-washy about it.

- *If one family prefers a "dry" reception and one family doesn't:* The reception should primarily reflect the side that is "hosting" the wedding. So if the bride and groom want to serve champagne and are paying for the bulk of the reception, but the bride's parents prefer that nothing harder than ginger beer gets poured, the bride and groom are entitled to the final word. Even in this age, when everyone is in recovery for something, people should be encouraged to govern themselves and not count on their hosts to keep them on track.
- *What about cash bars?* Cash bars are unfortunate. While they are relatively common in some regions, that doesn't make them a good idea. There is something fundamentally problematic about inviting people to an event and then making them pay for their food or drink or some part of the entertainment. This is a wedding reception, not a charity benefit, and guests are guests. They should not have to pay.

- *But I can't afford an open bar!* Open bars are expensive, and this is certainly an obvious area where one can trim one's budget if it is necessary. As with food selection, wedding hosts are not expected to fulfill every beverage fantasy their guests might have. They can decide to serve only wine and beer, or champagne and wine, or sparkling wine (like a Prosecco) and wine. They could really limit choices by serving champagne only for toasts or by creating a signature cocktail and having that be the alcoholic offering. It is always possible to find ways to be gracious within one's means.
- *My [uncle/aunt/fiancé's friend/formerly fun neighbor] drinks too much.* If this happens, the lush's behavior won't reflect poorly on you, really, but the antics of the soused can be annoying. If you know someone is going to be trouble, you don't have to ignore the problem. Tell the waitstaff to keep an eye on the problem person, and give them permission to cut him or her off. You can also clue in another friend or relative, who could run interference as well.

Who Needs Seating Charts? (or, I'm No Fascist)

One of the quirks of modern life is that people, in their private lives, have a hard time making demands that don't seem, from the outset, to have a greater point. Telling one's guests where to sit at one's wedding reception, for instance, can seem like a strangely controlling gesture at a party where you want things to be free and easy.

In truth, depending on the size and nature of the crowd, seating plans have all kinds of advantages. With guest lists composed of people who know only the bride and groom but few other people, they can encourage conversation. They can separate family members who would otherwise seek each other out to perpetuate ancient and boring arguments. There are also people in this world with the singular talent of being able to make deft conversation with brick walls, who can be used to draw out shy types with some strategic seating. The seating plan is a powerful tool and shouldn't be rejected out of hand. Sure, it takes work and time to put it together, but usually the sweat is worth it.

One way to facilitate good conversation is to pick one person or couple to "anchor" each table. The "anchor" people can be honored family members or life-of-the-party types, depending on what the situation requires. Then the rest of the table can be populated with an assortment of people who (1) know the anchors, (2) would be interested or amused by the anchors, (3) have something in common with the anchors that could spark chatter. This plan doesn't necessarily obviate the Bride's Table or Parents' Table, but it allows for some more flexibility, and does allow you to reject those tables if you don't want them. If, say, the bride's parents had a bitter divorce, or you know the grandparents will get along like the Hatfields and the McCoys, then consider mixing and matching at different tables (none with the bride and groom), and surround them with people who will find them entertaining.

Favoring

Wedding favors were once something couples would do only if they were seriously motivated by their culture (candied almonds are common wedding favors in Greek, Middle Eastern, Italian, and French traditions, among others), or because something seemed too appropriate to pass up (bottles of wine for guests when the wedding was at a vineyard, for instance). As with so many small nuptial gestures, once the Wedding-Industrial Complex became aware of the wedding favor, it became a "must." It isn't. Guests never know what to do with nonconsumable wedding favors, and the wedding couple, unless genuinely moved to have them, really doesn't need to spend the money or creative energy coming up with something novel that will, dollars to doughnuts, get forgotten in a rental car at the airport.

When It Isn't an Honor

Weddings often inspire brides and grooms to come up with weird "honor positions" that turn out to be more insulting than if the recruits had just been allowed to be "civilian" guests. It all seems so innocent and natural: There is a job to do, and one or the other member of the wedding couple feels guilty about having to leave someone out of the wedding party, but really, telling someone to be in charge of the guest book or some other task is insulting. These jobs pull whoever has to do them out of the fun part of the wedding reception—instead of being able to hang out and chat or get gently soused or dance with abandon, the friend (or relative) will always have to be taking care of something. Inevitably, if the person neglects the job, the wedding couple feels let down and furious because they trusted the person with the "honor" of the task.

At a certain point, it is worth acknowledging that many honors are just work and the chore can be spread around. The wedding party can take turns chaperoning the guest book, for instance, or the thing can just be passed from table to table at the reception. The key, really, is to let guests enjoy themselves without obligations.

Policing Toasts

Raucous guests, even the ones who are not hard of hearing, often confuse "toasts" with "roasts" and take the opportunity to trot out embarrassing stories about the bride in her heyday, when she would drink six vodka gimlets before doing something regrettable, or the groom's numerous previous paramours, who all had interesting talents. Can these blabbermouths be stopped?

The key is to plan ahead. If you are worried about loudmouths, decide who you want to perform toasts and ask them ahead of time. It is also possible to assign a friend or a musician to function as a kind of emcee who can do the dirty work of gently cutting people off if they threaten to run on, or start playing music as a cue to get people dancing, not listening.

If you're a guest and you sense you will be moved to propose a toast, it can't hurt to ask before the wedding if there is time for additional speakers. And as a general matter, if you *know* that your friends are shy and dislike public humiliation, restrain your comic impulses for a moment when they will be more appreciated.

Throwing

It is never necessary to throw anything at a wedding—not the bouquet, not a garter, not rice, not rose petals, not birdseed. If none of this is appealing, skip it.

If, on the other hand, you're amused by the bouquet toss, or its ilk, be fair about it. Don't exclude friends because you find them unattractive or because they're gay or because you don't approve of their dating styles or for any other reason that sucks the fun out of everything—the game should be open to anyone who is interested.

Money-Making Schemes

Certain wedding traditions were born out of genuine need—the wedding shower, for example, is a party that was created in order for the bride to be prepared to take on the duties of running a house, while other more recent developments seem to have more to do with greed. Occasionally people are inspired to introduce cash games—where the money goes to the bride and groom—into receptions, and this almost always feels uncomfortable. The two most popular cash gambits are the "dollar dance" and the "money tree." In the dollar dance, male guests are expected to pay to dance with the bride. Money trees are little strategically placed treelike structures that guests are supposed to adorn with cash. These are games that do have places in certain cultural traditions, and if you come from a region or family that celebrates with them, you don't need to worry so much.

But for most people, expecting any sort of financial exchange for the nuptial entertainment is unpleasant, as is treating the bride like a low-end stripper. No one should throw a wedding reception with the hope of making money off of it or breaking even. This is a party, not a benefit. Guests shouldn't be asked to donate to the "cause" of helping the bride and groom turn a profit on their wedding.

Party Stacking

Guest lists almost invariably fall prey to budgetary restrictions, but rather than accept this as a way of life, dedicated brides and grooms try to find ways of having it all. One questionable option is to have an "intimate" wedding ceremony and reception, which is immediately followed by a large-scale, food-free bash for the masses of friends who—for financial reasons—had to be excluded from the first half of the proceedings.

There are problems with this scheme. When parties are held back-to-back in this way, it will be impossible for the big group of nonintimate friends not to notice their second-class status. Even if they understand they are not part of the inner circle, it can still be rather insulting to know that a different crowd has been wined and dined until just before you were told to show up.

There is some tradition for having large numbers of people invited to the wedding ceremony and a more selective group asked to the reception (you can see examples of invitations to the ceremony only, or to the reception only, in chapter 8, "In Print: Wedding Stationery and What to Write on It"), but the stacked reception, where one group is worthy of being fed and the other isn't, is almost guaranteed to hurt feelings.

A much better plan is to have two entirely separate parties, either at different ends of the day (wedding in the morning with intimate lunch reception and wild bash in the evening) or in different weeks or months—anything to keep the "B" crowd from experiencing that horrible feeling of walking in and knowing that they missed the fun, or at least the tasty, stuff.

Etiquette in Action

FEEDING EVERYONE

Dear Elise,

My boyfriend and I are faced with a bunch of wedding issues, most of which arise from the facts that my family lives abroad, and his family are Orthodox Jews. We're finding reception food to be a sticking point.

His family keeps kosher, and it is traditional to have a meat meal for a festive occasion. I am a pescetarian, although I could live with a choice of fish or meat for the main course. Serving meat precludes *any* dairy. The crucial thing, however, is that kosher catering where we live is really awful, and even if we have a "dairy" reception, almost anything from these caterers (except for one or two upscale and out-of-budget restaurants) is really horrible. Can we have our cake and eat it too?

—Picky Palate

Dear Picky,

It is fascinating how so many wedding struggles are expressed through the menu. Vegans and vegetarians must balance their own gustatory interests and politics with those of their guests and family; parents often make the reception into an arena in which they try to grab control; and of course there are the complications of merging guests who keep kosher or have other religious dietary restrictions with those for whom anything goes.

Don't despair. There are many ways you can compromise on the meal. First, it would not be at all unusual or awkward for you to supply kosher meals for those who keep kosher and regular meals for the rest of your guests. (This may allow you to afford the fancier, tastier kosher meals because you are getting fewer of them.)

Should you go the individual meal route, there are certain steps to be aware of. The kosher caterer or restaurant should prepare the meals in accordance with kosher laws and deliver them wrapped in aluminum foil. The meals must stay wrapped until they are placed in front of the kosher-keeping guests, who then unwrap them themselves. This ensures that nothing nonkosher can come into contact with the food.

The cake issue also presents you with choices. You can get two cakes, one regular and one kosher, or you can forgo a kosher cake and serve kosher desserts. Again, you'll have to keep all serving utensils separate, but there is no reason you can't accommodate everyone.

Don't let yourself feel hemmed in by the notion that everyone will have to eat the same meal and follow the same dietary guidelines. That is the way of madness. Be flexible, and if anyone puts up resistance, point out that you have already compromised (on the meat issue). In a wedding, everyone has to bend a little to prevent any one person from breaking.

PAYING FOR DRINKS

Dear Elise,

We are trying to plan a wedding that best fits our budget and unfortunately, this will mean eliminating an open bar. Is it all right if we have a cash bar, considering that many of the people we are inviting also had cash bars at their weddings? Someone suggested that we buy a few cases of champagne and have bottles at the tables instead of a cash bar, which we could afford.

—Concerned About Booze

Dear CAB,

While cash bars have recently gained some tolerance in some places, etiquette truly frowns upon the entire notion of making guests pay for their food and drink. I agree that it's a bad practice. If one has a party, one pays for one's guests.

There is also no reason that anyone should ever spend more than one has to throw a party, nor is there any reason to think that one must cater to every desire one's guests might have. So if you can't afford an open bar, but you can purchase some cases of wine or champagne (or some of each), then you can limit your alcohol options that way. This is not an uncommon route to take, so if you choose to do this, don't think you are doing anything weird or provocative.

Being gracious does not mean bankrupting yourself or accommodating every possible desire of every single guest. It is being kind and friendly and nontaxing. A reception should not come with financial strings attached.

FACILITIES

Dear Elise,

I am planning a wedding in the country at my grandfather's farm. The barns have some refrigerators, room for a bar, and all sorts of cool old-fashioned farming equipment. I love the idea of renting a tent and having my wedding there. The only problem is that there is no plumbing.

The guest list is quite large, and I know I'd have to rent some Porta Potties, but will people—especially the older relatives—be angry about having to use such facilities? How will older relatives handle this? How will I handle it in a wedding dress?

—Barn Bash

Dear BB,

Your grandfather sounds like a hell of a guy and if he's offering, that is one terrific reception location. As far as the delicate question of Porta Potties goes, your primary obligation as host is to provide some sort of washroom facility, the relative luxury of which is really determined by location. In other words, it would probably not come as an enormous surprise to your guests that you had to bring in temporary plumbing for a wedding and reception in and around some barns. As long as they are clean, you've done the job. It is true that some of your older guests might be startled by the portable toilets, so in a few cases you may want to warn them ahead of time, not to dissuade them from coming but to let them know what to expect. You could also look into renting handicapped-accessible facilities for guests who might need (and appreciate) such amenities.

The question of your dress is not one of etiquette but of practicality, temperament, and fashion. If you end up wearing a large dress with a complicated train or bustle that could easily get dirty, or if you wear something that demands secure assistance before using the bathroom, you might be in for a long night. A simpler, perhaps tea-length, dress might be a more Porta Potti–friendly option. All you have to decide is what will make you most comfortable and most able to have a good time.

SOME DRINK, OTHERS DON'T

Dear Elise,

My parents, who are paying for our wedding, are strict about not drinking. They have offered to host two receptions: one with finger foods and punch for all of our guests immediately following the ceremony, and a small, "close friends and family" dinner later in the evening, where a moderate amount of alcohol would be served. I would like to have one wedding reception during which we could serve wine or champagne, and my fiancé's family expects to have alcohol served. Our reception site offers bar prices by the hour or per drink charged to the wedding, not to the guests. Would it be wrong for us to ask his parents to cover the costs of alcohol? I can't ask my parents to pay for a bar, but I don't want to insult his family. My fiancé and I have been dreading this issue from day one of wedding planning.

—Alcohol Conflict

Dear Alcohol Conflict,

You must figure out whether your parents simply don't want to pay for alcohol or if they truly don't want people drinking at all. If it is a question of cost alone, then you could approach your fiancé's parents and explain the situation to them. It would then be up to them whether or not to pick up the bar tab.

If your parents are fundamentally opposed to alcohol and do not want an open bar at any party they host, then you have a different set of issues to negotiate. If this is the case, and they are unwilling to bend, there is little you can do if they are paying for the event and feel they have already compromised. (This compromise of serving only wine, by the way, is one that many people decide upon as a way to economize. As long as there is enough wine or champagne for guests to drink, there is no reason you need to feel uncomfortable about not serving hard alcohol.)

If your fiancé's family is determined to have an open-bar celebration, perhaps they could take matters into their own hands and host a rehearsal dinner or cocktail event. This will allow both families to celebrate in the manner to which they have become accustomed, while maintaining a spirit of compromise. You will have to be gentle with both sets of parents, and it may take some coaxing to get people to be frank about what they will and will not live with. Compromise is always possible, though you may have to relegate the drinking to a night when your parents are not footing the bill.

ONE BRIDESMAID DUTY TOO MANY?

Dear Elise,

I am going to be a bridesmaid in my friend's extremely traditional wedding. The bride is insisting that we dance the first dance with our "partners." I feel uncomfortable dancing with some stranger when my husband is going to be a guest, and I'd rather dance with him. What should I do?

—Reluctant Bridesmaid

Dear Reluctant,

Where do you draw the line as a bridesmaid? Is it at the expensive dress you probably won't wear again? Is it at the bachelorette party you don't want to host? For you, the sticking point is over whether, in the name of friendship, you should dance one dance with someone who is not your husband. Is this issue really that big a deal? How long is the dance number going to be, anyway? Four minutes? Five?

Of course, if it is really a huge issue for you, it isn't out of the question for you to ask your friend if you could dance with your husband instead of your arranged partner (this would be a groomsman, I take it). But really, people do all sorts of silly things for their friends when they're members of a wedding party. Some of these jobs are unpleasant, and others are unpleasant and expensive. This one is free, brief, and leaves you open to dance with your husband for the rest of the evening. Is it worth fussing over?

MOTHERS AND THE DANCE CARD

Dear Elise,

I was raised by my birth mother *and* by my father and stepmother. I love both of the women who brought me up, but they don't get along with each other. I would like to have a mother-son dance with each of them, and I want to make sure that they both feel important. Do I dance with each of them for half a song or have separate dances? Which one should I dance with first? How can I let my mother know I want to dance with my stepmother, too?

—Confused

Dear Confused,

Divide and conquer. The safest way to deal with this dance situation is to come up with a plan that gives each of these women a chance to be in the spotlight with you. Once you decide what you want to do, tell your mother and stepmother, but don't invite discussion. You want to protect yourself and you want to protect them from each other, so neither should have a sense that either got treated with any kind of preference.

The best solution is to have two entirely separate dances, and you could invite your mother and stepmother to collaborate with you on picking their songs. This way you have included them and given them some autonomy, but you haven't relinquished control over a touchy situation. As for who goes first, I think it would be fair for you to give preference to your biological mother, but then you should find a moment, perhaps after toasts or immediately after cake cutting or at some other natural break in things, to showcase your dance with your stepmother. You want to preserve everyone's goodwill, and to do that you have to coddle.

When breaking the news to your mother, there's no way to control her reaction, but again you can present your decision as a fait accompli and not open to negotiation. Telling her that your dance with her will be first and not happen back-to-back with the one you will do with your stepmother should give you some ammunition.

DANCING WITH MULTIPLE DADS

Hello Elise,

I have two dads, and I don't know how to handle the walk down the aisle and the father-daughter dance. I get along okay with my biological father, but my legal father (my stepfather adopted me) is the one I've grown up with. My relationships with both men aren't great. What should I do about these traditions?

—What's Reasonable?

Dear What's Reasonable,

You don't mention what *you* want to do about these traditions. Do you have a preference at all? Would you rather not walk down the aisle or dance with either of them? You can always settle this problem by opting out. No one will arrest you for skipping these traditions.

If you aren't comfortable with passive resistance, consider walking down the aisle with both men, or have your mother escort you if you two are close. As for dancing, remember that the bride-and-dad dances are not held alone in a spotlight. Traditionally, other people are out on the dance floor by the time the bride dances with her father.

You could also sit down with each man and ask him to pick a song for your dance. In this way, you will give each one a bit of personalized ego stroking while avoiding, again, the entire notion of having to give one man "better treatment" than the other. As to which one goes first, I think you can assert your own slight preference, but there's no reason you shouldn't give preference to your biological father for the sake of simplicity, or, if they're extremely petty, you could tell them you'll take them in alphabetical order.

Chapter 15

Do I Have To? Thank-You Notes

Do you have to? Yes, you do. Every wedding present, from the most expensive to the least comprehensible, requires a thank-you note. They seem like such little, forgettable things, since they contain primarily polite, generic, and obvious information, but their actual purpose is something more substantial: They provide closure in the way they specifically and personally acknowledge each gift giver's participation in the wedding.

Traditional Basics

- Thank-you notes must be prompt. Ideally, they are written as soon as the present has been opened and its origins and purpose identified.
- All notes should be written and sent within three months of the wedding—unless the presents themselves arrived longer after the fact.
- The body of the note should mention the present.
- Stationery is significant. Do not use fill-in-the-blank cards. If desired, two sets of cards can be ordered, one with the bride's "maiden" initials for

prewedding missives and the other with the bride's married initials (if they are changing) for postwedding thank-you notes. It is also reasonable to use blank note cards.

- Do not use preprinted cards that say how grateful you are for the thoughtful gift. These things need to be original, sincere, personalized, and handwritten.
- Traditionally, brides have been in charge of writing thank-you cards. But there is no reason grooms can't pick up the slack.
- There is some tradition of addressing thank-you notes to the female half of the couple, since it is presumed that she will have been the one selecting and sending the present in the first place. This is condescending and no longer necessary.
- If the present is hideous, there is no reason to be unpleasant. It is, after all, still a present, and therefore should be nicely acknowledged.

Twisting Tradition

There is no way around the thank-you-note tradition. So set aside the fact that this isn't a thrilling chore in the way that, say, sorting laundry or changing the cat's litter box is. It has its rewards, and it is no longer a job one person needs to tackle alone.

Share the Job

Men have gotten off easy in the thank-you-note department for decades, if not centuries. Considering the emphasis and importance that is placed on sending these missives, it seems a bit shabby to leave a significant job to only half of the married couple. Both parties should pitch in. Among the unacceptable excuses for not writing notes are:

- "I don't know them as well as you do."
- "That is a kitchen present, and I don't like to cook as much as you do."
- "They'll be expecting a note from the *wife*."
- "You're a better writer than I am."
- "My handwriting is bad."
- "I don't even know what that thing is. How can I thank someone for it?"

They have to be done, and it doesn't matter who does them.

No, You Don't Have a Year

A rumor blossomed out of nowhere that one has a year in which to write thank-you notes, just as guests have a year in which to send the presents in the first place. This isn't true, and it wouldn't be desirable if it were. People will wonder if their presents arrived, they will be irritated that their gifts were never acknowledged, and their hard feelings will not be mitigated by a fake "rule" that suggests that the thank-you-note window is longer than a human pregnancy.

The key to making thank-you-note writing bearable is to write and send them as the presents come in. Letting them pile up until they become a hulking mass that laughs at you when you think you have nothing to do on a Sunday morning is an act of masochism. Each note takes five minutes to write, while a stack of twenty becomes a task that inspires bad moods and writer's cramp.

They Gave Me Cash. What Do I Say?

People may hope desperately for gifts of money, but they never know quite how to be gracious and not somehow crass in acknowledging them. The key is to be cheerful and just a little bit coy. One never needs to mention amounts or be specific; you can just say "thank you for your generous gift," and then it always helps to elaborate by saying what the money may pay for: "It has been earmarked for a new sofa we've been coveting," or "it will help us make a down payment on our house." There is no need to go into extreme detail, but friends and family will appreciate the sense that their money is being put toward some fundamental aspect of the couple's "new" life together.

I Hate It

Inevitably, in spite of all your best efforts, something horrible will show up on your doorstep. While you don't have to lie and say that the present is something you've long been dreaming about, many of the phrases that traditional etiquette offers as useful ways to disguise disgust are actually very revealing. Everyone knows that you are speaking in code if you call a present "interesting" and that you're actually being sort of unpleasant, which isn't really the point of the thank-you note.

Your best bet is to be gracious and thank the person for thinking of you and for taking the care to pick the thing, whatever it was, out for you. Then you can change the subject and say how nice it was to see your friend or relative at the wedding or how great it will be to see him or her or them in the future.

Everyone Gets Thanked

Sometimes groups of people pool their resources for one big present. It may seem like an injustice, but everyone in the group deserves a separate thank-you note.

When to Ask

Where's that present? This is a question that gift givers and potential recipients ask with some frequency, given that not everyone is quick on the draw when it comes to sending wedding presents and thank-you notes alike.

If you've sent a present and are wondering whether it reached the bride and groom, it is absolutely reasonable to ask. Don't pounce on them if you haven't received a note within days of sending your gift, since that will just make you seem petty and make your friends feel guilty and put-upon, but if a few months have gone by with no mention of the present and you're wondering what happened to it, ask gently. Don't say, "Since I *never got a thank-you note from you,* I'm just wondering . . . ," since for obvious reasons you would come off as twisting the knife a bit. Merely ask, as part of a larger conversation, if your present got to its destination and leave it at that.

The other side of things is a bit more delicate. If you are a newlywed, wondering whether or not someone gave you something, you are not in a position to ask. There's no way to do it without looking grabby. The only possible exception to this policy is if you have somehow received confirmation (from a store, for instance) that a present has been sent by these people, and you have yet to see it. That is a practical concern you can definitely look into, but anything you feel is a general lapse is probably just that. Prompting for presents will only make you seem greedy, so it's best to simply give up on the idea of seeing gifts from some people. Take comfort in the fact that they have given you the gift of one less thank-you note to write.

=======   *Etiquette in Action*   =======

TYPED THANK-YOU NOTES

Hi Elise,

Due to a physical handicap, I am unable to write notes by hand. Would it be acceptable for me to use personalized stationery with typed thank-you notes? Many guests will be from my family, and I do not want to make my husband handwrite notes to people he doesn't know.

—Eye Issues

Dear Eye Issues,

While it is customary for thank-you notes to be handwritten, you have an obvious reason why this is physically not feasible for you. You can absolutely type your correspondence.

You mention not wanting your husband to have to write to people he may have never met, and this is fair of you, but I feel obliged to point out that thank-you-note composition is traditionally something the new wife does, and historically she would often find herself writing little missives to people she may never have met. It is not unreasonable for contemporary couples to share thank-you-note responsibilities, so you wouldn't be wrong if you received some help with the notes.

POSTAL SERVICE SPOILS PROMPTNESS

Dear Elise,

I got married months ago, and the post office just returned a pile of slightly destroyed thank-you notes I'd written just weeks after the wedding. How can I convey what happened in my replacement notes so my guests won't think I'm rude?

—ARRRGH

Dear ARRRGH,

While it is true that no one likes a lame excuse, there's nothing wrong with telling the truth and having a sense of humor. All you can do is seize your pen and stamps and send out new thank-you notes as soon as you can. Feel free to mention the post office snafu, and make amends for the delay by being more personal in your new letters. Since a chunk of time has passed, you may actually have more to say about the presents than when they first arrived into your life. Did you get a cocktail shaker that enabled you to concoct a fabulous New Year's drink? Perhaps someone gave you a blanket that is keeping you snug this winter? Here's a chance to elaborate a little bit. Certainly you're embarrassed, but as long as you send those letters out pronto, you'll be square with the world.

HOW TO SIGN

Dear Elise,

My husband and I have been writing thank-you cards. Because my handwriting is neater than my husband's, I wrote out the cards and signed them with both my first and last name and then passed them to my husband for him to sign his own name. When my husband saw I had included my last name, he asked me why, and I told him I did it because I saw the thank-you card as a way to announce our names. My husband thinks that anyone who knows us knows that my last name is the same as it was before marriage, and he signed only his first name. So now we have some cards with my full name and only his first. He has no problem with me not changing my name; he just thinks it will make the cards less personal to put our full names on them. What is proper?

—Confused Thank-You

Dear Confused,

You want your thank-you notes to multitask. In general, thank-you notes for wedding presents are informal. It is customary for one to sign only one's first name at the bottom of thank-you notes, unless one isn't well acquainted with the person being thanked. (If you get a present, for instance, from one of your parents' coworkers, you may have to provide more identifying information.)

At worst, you may seem a little stiff and overly formal in your notes, which is hardly a disaster. Consider how you might react if a good friend wrote to you with such a formal signature. It isn't insulting, just a bit odd.

Your desire to let people know that you are keeping your name is reasonable, but it is unlikely that people will register this information through your signature. If you were at the beginning of the process, you could take advantage of a couple of ways to make your stationery proclaim your names for you. You could order some cards with both your name and your husband's name printed on them, and use them for all your thank-you correspondence, or you could send at-home cards, which seem old-fashioned but also get your point across. Seeing your name in print would solidify it in your friends' minds.

For now, you can send out the cards you've written with your full name on them and your husband's first name only—and adopt a less formal policy from here on out. It is unlikely that your guests will compare notes, so don't worry.

TRAUMA AND THANK-YOU NOTES

Dear Elise,

My thank-you notes are really late. My husband and I have been married for a year, and I haven't written any yet. Everything from house-ruining natural disasters to serious illness landed on us this year, and I've just been too exhausted to deal with them. I am trying to let people know that we have been overwhelmed. Most of our guests were very generous, but some didn't give us anything. Someone even gave us a check that bounced. Do I send a thank-you card?

—Traumatized

Dear Traumatized,

First, you should write and send all of your thank-you notes. Extremely late is still better than not at all. Apologize for the lateness and briefly acknowledge your chaotic year before moving on to the "thank you" part of your note.

In order to get through them without losing your mind, don't try writing them all at once. Set yourself a goal of doing a few a day and put them in the mail as soon as you have written them.

Every present, no matter how small or odd, deserves a note. In the case of the bounced check, you should also write. The relative surely knows that the check was returned and is certainly embarrassed. It is difficult to tactfully discuss the fact that the check bounced, so tread lightly. At the very least, you can thank your friend or relative for thinking of you.

As for the people who didn't give you presents at all, just be happy that you have fewer notes to write.

STATIONERY QUIBBLE

Hi Elise,

We're getting thank-you note cards printed that have our names on the front of them. If I receive a present individually, through the bridal shower, is it okay for me to send the thank-you note on our joint name cards, or should I use different cards?

—Gearing Up

Dear Gearing,

The key to thank-you-note happiness is to get them out of your house as quickly as you can. To that end, stationery doesn't matter, and you can use any sort of card you like. You are perhaps breaking with tradition somewhat if you use your joint name cards before your wedding, but the minor protocol violation is nothing compared to the virtue in a quick response.

THEY NEVER GOT SENT

Dear Elise,

A relative was briefly married. She and her ex-husband married and divorced amidst some serious health problems for her, and in all the fuss she didn't send many of her thank-you notes.

What should she do? She isn't even sure who got thank-you notes and who didn't, or even who gave what. It is awkward to address things now, but she doesn't want anyone to feel slighted.

—To Thank or Not to Thank

Dear To Thank,

Your relative has a complicated situation on her hands, and I hope she has recovered both from her illness and her marriage. She is right that she should acknowledge her friends and the presents they gave her at the time. Her marriage did, after all, occur, and presents were given and people did attend. Presumably, her friends and family understand what she has been through, so she should try to reconstruct as best she can who gave what, and send out acknowledgments. In the cases where it is impossible to figure out what was given by whom, she can still send a note, apologizing for her silence and thanking her guests for supporting her at the wedding and being so generous. She does not need to go into complicated justifications; it would just be nice and brave of her to thank her friends.

WAITING ON SPECIAL STATIONERY?

Dear Elise,

My wedding shower and my bachelorette party were held only a few days before my wedding. Should I write separate thank-you notes for the shower and wedding presents? It seems weird to write a thank-you note for the shower gift without mentioning the wedding gift that arrived. At the same time, the shower gifts are from the women only, while the wedding gifts are often from a couple, so it would be odd to thank half the couple for a present he had nothing to do with. Also, our graphic designer friend offered to make us thank-you cards, but they won't be finished for at least three weeks. I already have some stationery. Would it be okay if I got started writing using my nonpersonalized cards?

—Gifted

Dear Gifted,

While it is a popular option, printing specialty thank-you cards often takes a lot of time, and the weight of the notes becomes oppressive as you wait for your stationery. If possible, for your own sake, you should just get a head start rather than wait.

You also do not need to be coy and pretend that you aren't aware that you got two presents from the same person, one at the shower and the other for the wedding. You can absolutely combine discussions of both presents in one note as long as you mention both items. If it makes you more comfortable, address your comments about the shower present specifically to the female half of the couple.

This might mean you end up writing slightly longer notes for the ones you double up on, but think of the savings in stamps.

<hr />

MYSTERY PRESENT

Hello Elise,

We received a lovely present—with no card. We had a large wedding, which makes it harder to track the giver down.

We're planning on sending thank-you notes on personalized stationery to everyone who came. Would it be proper to preprint a line such as "P.S. We received a beautiful glass bowl without a card. Was it from you? Let us know so that we can thank you!" Or is that crass?

—No ID

Dear No ID,

Presents suffer from lost (and sometimes stolen) identities all the time. As a general matter, it is unwise to discuss the particulars of one's presents in global correspondence. These are not subtle times, but the reasons for this are subtle. Putting such information into print would be taking a private matter and making it public.

There are two routes you can take. One is to play detective and see if you can work backward by calling the store that wrapped the gift up and shipped it. If that fails, another stealthy approach is to examine your guest list, cross off all the people who gave other presents (or who you can discount for other reasons), and then make some strategic calls or e-mails. You don't have to be coy. Just say that you have an orphaned present that you love and ask if they know who might have sent it, because you want to send a thank-you note. With any luck, and some psychological profiling, you shouldn't have to quiz too many people.

THANK-YOU NOTES FOR GROUP PRESENT

Dear Elise,

We are wondering how to compose a thank-you note for a group present. One of my husband's relatives came to our wedding accompanied by one of his three children (we didn't invite his other two children), and he gave us a present with a card saying that the present was from all four members of the family. Writing separate notes to each of them (they don't live together) seems awkward, since only two of the four were invited. My husband thinks we should write notes only to the two who attended our wedding. I think we should send a single thank-you to the family, at the father's address. What should we do?

—Group Gift Dilemma

Dear Group Gift Dilemma,

In this case, you're best off facing your fears directly and sending thank-you notes to each of the four gift givers. If all of them pitched in on a present for you, they certainly all deserve to be thanked directly.

As for discomfort, if you are certain that the two people who were not invited did not mind being excluded, then you truly have no reason to hesitate. The right thing to do is to thank each person directly for his or her participation in your present. I know it means some extra writing, but your graciousness will be noted if you send everyone a personal thank-you.

Chapter 16

Coping with the Worst: Postponement, Disownment, Cancellation, Disillusion

There are plenty of pessimists in the world who dutifully conjure worst-case scenarios for every happy event and imagine ways to brace for disaster. For others, such dark fantasies are idiotic and merely a waste of time that could be better spent perfecting one's original vows, wrestling over the seating chart, or sleeping. Lightning can strike regardless of whether or not its victim is a glass-half-full type. Etiquette—traditional and otherwise—will never take the pain out of unrequited love or parents behaving horribly or the embarrassment of having to admit that the stars just weren't aligned, but it can provide a path toward something that is useful both for the public face and for the spirit of getting on with life: dignity.

Traditional Basics

Standard etiquette does not make romantic recommendations or offer detailed solutions on how to get parents to behave like the adults their birth certificates suggest they are. It instead reminds everyone about the difference between the public and the private, and that even in these days where people confess to everything on television, there is no obligation to tell all.

Tradition offers only a few suggestions for protocol when one is under terrible circumstances:

- *Parental disapproval:* If one or both sets of parents refuse to give permission or their "blessing" for the marriage, the wedding can still take place, as long as the bride and groom are of legal age. They must not, however, count on receiving any support from the doubting parents.

- *Broken engagements and love tokens:* As a general matter, the engagement ring and any other love tokens should be returned to the giver. (This ensures that any heirlooms will stay with the family of origin.) Some say that the engagement ring should stay with the un-bride if her fiancé was the one to call off the relationship, but the best way to handle this sort of heartbreak is to return everything and start afresh. (Of course, if the giver is gracious enough to want his or her ex to keep it, that arrangement is more than civilized.)

- *Broken engagements and other presents:* Engagement presents should be returned with a brief, circumspect note of explanation saying that the wedding will not be taking place. Traditional etiquette, never flinching from the morbid, does make an exception for brides (though this policy should apply to grooms as well) whose fiancés have died: If encouraged by the present givers, they may keep the presents they have received.

- *Broken engagements and newspaper announcements:* If the engagement was announced in a newspaper, the publication should be notified. A simple note saying that the engagement has been broken "by mutual consent," without any further explanation, does the job perfectly well. Depending on the timing, the newspaper either will not publish the original engagement announcement or, if the announcement has already been printed, it can publish this new development. (Perhaps because of how changeable engagements can be, many newspapers now only publish wedding announcements after the fact.)

- *Postponed wedding:* Depending on when and how the wedding has been postponed, there are a few bits of protocol to observe. Presents do not need to be returned unless the "postponement" is really a cancellation.

- If a wedding has to be postponed at the last minute, the only thing to do is call all the prospective guests and explain that the nuptials have been put off and they don't have to get their fancy clothes dry-cleaned just yet.

- If invitations have been sent and a wedding has to be postponed for a specific reason (a death in the family, a natural disaster), it is *optional* to include that information on a new announcement—assuming there is time to send one out. It would look like this:

Mr. Henry Farber and Ms. Violet Katz

regret that

OPTIONAL: [owing to a death in the family / hurricane / tsunami / illness]

the marriage of their daughter

Felice

to

Mr. Ronald Dawson

has been postponed [to]

OPTIONAL: [new date if one has been selected]

º If invitations have been printed but not yet sent, and the new date is known, then an additional card can be included with the original invitation (with the original date crossed out):

<blockquote>
Kindly note that

the date of the wedding has been changed

to

Saturday, the seventeenth of March

at five o'clock
</blockquote>

• *Canceled wedding:* This is indeed unfortunate—the more so because it is a private matter that must be made excruciatingly public.

º If there is time to do a mailing before prospective guests get on airplanes, an announcement can be sent out, reading:

<blockquote>
Mr. and Mrs. Sean Carlton

announce that the marriage of

their daughter

Martha

to

Mr. Benjamin Coffee

will not take place.
</blockquote>

º If there is no time to mail an announcement, all guests must be contacted personally. There is never any need to shower people with explanatory information, even if they are desperate for it.

- *Very brief marriage:* Occasionally it happens that couples wake up after the fact and realize they should have quit while they were ahead. At this point, dissolving the marriage is all that is necessary. No one is required to send out announcements, and the wedding presents do not have to be returned. Traditionally, the soon-to-be ex-bride keeps the wedding gifts, but to be fair, the wedding presents are part of the common property of the marriage. They can be divided according to interest or need or as equally as possible.

Twisting Tradition

There's plenty that's easier said than done about keeping a stiff upper lip when everything falls apart, but keep in mind that the world does not need to be privy to your most intimate details and that part of getting married under a cloud, breaking an engagement, or getting unmarried is that in moments of discomfort, hiding behind a curtain of discretion and civility can only work in your favor.

You Can't Disown Me, I Quit!

Parents can disapprove of their children's matches. They're entitled. Of course, the kids in question can go ahead and get married, however and whenever and to whomever they like, provided they're on solid legal ground. What remains is the question of whether there is any willingness to get along after the wedding. If parents wave the dread "disownment" over their kids, they should expect their bluff will be called.

How does one handle horrible parents? Establish a degree of dignity and try to be more civilized than they are. If they are maintaining an angry silence, it can only stand you in good stead to send them invitations. It is, after all, much better for you to be able to point to a concrete example of how you made an effort than it will be for them to say that they rejected you. On the other hand, if they are consistently vindictive and threatening, there is nothing wrong with giving them fair warning ("This is a happy day for me, and while I want you to celebrate with me, I can't invite you if you're going to act so badly") and proceeding accordingly.

There is a key to how recalcitrant parents and angry children can handle unwelcome nuptials: Ditch the politics. A wedding isn't the place to try to make global relationship readjustments. Hold your tongue. Be polite. See if the new union and the end of the wedding haze don't encourage more closeness generally. If they don't, you gave it a shot and you can feel comfortable about maintaining a reasonable distance from the people who make you unhappy going forward.

How Do I Explain . . .

If you postpone or cancel a wedding, expect everyone—regardless of how close or distant, regardless of whether or not they were even invited or could possibly care—to demand the dirt on your situation. If you don't want to talk about it, you aren't obliged to spill.

When faced with the uncomfortably direct questions, you can fall back on a few stock responses. Of course, these are all transparent euphemisms, but their purpose is only to fill the gaping hole left by an intrusive question. And you can always change the subject immediately.

- If you postponed, and the reason is very complicated, but you're still getting married: "There were so many problems with that date, that we just decided to pick something more convenient."

- If your parents refuse to attend the wedding: "I don't know what their plans are, but of course I invited them and I hope they can make it."
- If one parent boycotts the wedding: "I don't know what's going on with him/her, but of course I would love to have him/her at the wedding."
- If you really don't want your parents at your wedding: "Oh, we'll do something private with them some other time."
- If you call off the whole thing: "We decided it was the wrong time to get married" or "We didn't feel right about things and didn't want to make a mistake that would be hard to undo."
- If your marriage was incredibly short: "We made a mistake and thought we should fix it as quickly as possible."

When Do I Break It Off?

Whether you want to postpone your wedding or break off the engagement entirely, the best bet is to make your move as soon as you've made up your mind. Waiting only makes cancellation more expensive and more embarrassing for all parties involved (including any traveling guests). Having said that, try not to time your breakup to coincide with enormously stressful events in your soon-to-be ex-partner's life (exams, holidays, medical procedures, family crises, heavy deadlines). Breaking up will take infinitely more sensitivity than forming your relationship did, so you will have to be patient and exercise the kind of care that might not come naturally, given the seismic shift in your feelings. If you have to fake it to be kind, do so, but don't string your partner along. That's not only rude, it's cruel.

What Do I Say?

There is a lot to be said for maintaining your dignity in the face of disaster (whether you are the jilter or the jiltee). Everyone will feel entitled to prod you for the details. Stick with the old standbys and don't elaborate too much unless you actually want to get into it. At this point, you don't want any more blood in the water, so try to let everything settle before you start trashing your ex, your ex's family, and anyone who ever thought your ex was cute or funny.

- In the case of a slow collapse: "Things just didn't work out."
- After a surprise jilting: "I don't know what happened, but at least we don't have to deal with getting divorced."
- If you broke it off: "Things weren't right, and it wouldn't have been fair to get married with so many problems."

What About the Presents?

The traditional policy—that one should return engagement and wedding gifts if one received them before a wedding that was canceled, while one is entitled to keep all the presents if the wedding actually happened (even if the marriage was very short)—is not a bad one. It draws firm lines that almost anyone can understand, and besides, who would want to get back a blender that someone has been using for months?

The bigger questions are about division of assets and general fairness. It is so easy to be petty, but really, your goal should be for maximum dignity and minimum contact with your ex (or soon-to-be ex). If a present was obviously meant for you (someone sent a gorgeous stand mixer and you're a master baker, while your ex can't handle microwaving a burrito properly), then you should be the one to keep it, but beyond those issues, try not to wrestle too much. Present haggling inspires the wrong kinds of passions when what you want is to be coolheaded and magnanimous.

This is especially the case when it comes to engagement rings (or other engagement presents). It is so much better all around if, when an engagement is broken, you at least try to return the ring *or* whatever other token has been given to you. If your ex wants you to keep the gift, that's another story, but the canceled engagement is a sign that you have to let go of the relationship, and that includes the ring or other significant objects. (The notable exceptions to this are if you bought the item yourself for yourself or if the ring is a family heirloom, in which case it really should remain with its original family.)

Who Deals with Canceling Everything?

Typically, the people who were supposed to host the defunct nuptials are in charge of handling the unpleasant aftermath—calling the vendors and seeing how much of their deposits can be recovered, contacting guests (by phone or through the mail, time permitting) and letting them know that they now have a free weekend, and managing all the other sundry necessities of damage control.

There are some notable strong souls who soldier on in the face of a canceled wedding and turn the reception into a starting-over party, and there have even been people who have heroically staged charity benefits on the ashes of their trashed nuptials. These options are always open, but you don't have to pursue them unless the spirit moves you.

It is also a gracious gesture for the breaker-upper to pitch in and help disassemble the wedding that wasn't, even if it means having to call dozens of people with the regrettable news.

The inevitable question of expenses is a hard one. Generally, deposits are lost when the event is canceled, and while it is a kind and civilized gesture for the breaker-upper to offer to reimburse the host or hosts for some of the lost money (unless, of course, the breaker-upper *is* the host or a child of the hosts), this sort of generosity is rare. At bottom, though, this is a situation where it is infinitely better to wash one's hands of the situation. Fighting over cash will only extend a relationship that really should end as quickly as possible.

=============   *Etiquette in Action*   =============

WHO GETS THAT RING?

Dear Elise,

I was engaged for a few months, and my boyfriend just broke things off and asked for the ring back. By law, am I required to return the ring, since he called off the engagement? I just want to know my rights in case it has to be determined in civil court.

—Need to Know

Dear Need to Know,

Sadly, the principles of etiquette do not govern those of our legal system. I could bliss out for hours over the peaceful possibilities of polite trials and lawsuits forgone because it is easier to forgive minor sins than to extract excessive revenge. But this is not the way of things. Consequently, I can't advise you on the legal ramifications of refusing to return your engagement ring. I do not even know where you reside, and the rules for these sorts of questions vary widely according to your legal jurisdiction.

Etiquette-wise, the policies are pretty clear on the question of rings (or other presents) and broken engagements. Return them. Some traditions say that if the giver breaks it off, he or she should not expect the item to be returned, but if the receiver breaks it off, it is a classy and civilized gesture to return it. Heirlooms should be returned to their family of origin. That is the only fair thing to do.

So, indeed, etiquette could say that you're entitled to keep the ring. But ask yourself if you're better off having protracted angry contact with your ex-fiancé and possibly having to drag this breakup out into a legal battle, or if you'd be happier returning the ring to this fellow who will surely not wear it, and so will either have a sad reminder of your relationship hanging around the house or take a financial loss on selling it?

See how you feel when the heat of your ire burns off a bit. You can always buy yourself another ring, one without unpleasant associations.

SHOULD PRESENTS BOOMERANG BACK?

Dear Elise,

What is the time limit you have to return wedding gifts if the marriage fails? I know someone who was married less than a year. Shouldn't she return the presents?

　　—Just Wondering

Dear Just Wondering,

Are you hoping that the present you selected will make a reappearance in your life? If so, I'm sorry to be the bearer of disappointing news.

If a wedding is canceled, presents should absolutely be returned, but once the deed is done, all bets are off. So even if the marriage doesn't last a year, or even a season, the gifts remain the possessions of the wedding couple and become elements in the unfortunate tug-of-war over "community property." Occasionally, if there is a quick annulment, presents are returned.

The alternatives are simply too strange. How long would it be necessary for a marriage to last before the wedding couple could really be said to own their presents? Would anyone really want to discover a much-used Cuisinart and a tearstained note explaining the collapse of a marriage in the mailbox? No. It is much better to leave all of this unsaid and simply feel sorry that such a happy occasion did not promise a happy union for your friend.

CANCELED WEDDING AND THE DRESS

Dear Elise,

I wanted to contribute some money toward my son's wedding, so I paid for his fiancée's wedding dress. Now the wedding is off. Should she return the dress the way she would return other wedding gifts?

—Not Yet a Mother-in-Law

Dear Not Yet,

This is an uncomfortable situation to be sure, and I'll offer you my condolences, unless you are relieved that everything fell apart when it did.

Indeed, the general policy when it comes to presents and canceled weddings is that the booty all goes back, and this would apply to the dress you bought for the bride as well. How you choose to approach this with your son's former fiancée is up to you. If she puts up a fight about it, it may be preferable just to wash your hands of the matter. What are you going to do with her unworn wedding dress anyway, if it is something that can't be returned? Be glad the expenses, both tangible and emotional, weren't higher, as they clearly would have been had the wedding happened.

HOW TO POSTPONE

Dear Elise,

My fiancé and I are considering postponing our wedding. We have not mailed our invitations yet, but a save-the-date card already went out. If we do postpone, how do we tell people? We want to maintain our privacy. And are we responsible for people's plane tickets?

—Cautious

Dear Cautious,

Whatever you do, don't cringe. The world could use more people capable of looking before leaping, and it is always one's prerogative to change, cancel, or postpone one's own wedding.

From an etiquette standpoint, all you are obliged to do is advise your guests as soon as you possibly can of the shift in plans. Any guest indiscreet enough to quiz you about your reasons deserves a classic nonanswer. Anything from "I'd rather not discuss it" to "This is what works best for us" will suffice. Do not let people bully you into giving them what they imagine will be juicy details. They will get a greater frisson out of imagining your reasons than actually knowing them, so why spoil their fun if it lets you maintain your privacy?

How you communicate your postponement is another matter. If you have time, you can send out cards that say your wedding has been postponed indefinitely. (You can even, if you're feeling up to it, tell everyone to stay tuned for a new date, time, and place.) If you are pressed for time and not inclined to do a mailing, you can telephone your guests and let them know that the wedding is off—for now. The disadvantages to the second course of action are twofold: You have to have a quick tongue and the ability not to get into the details with everyone you call, and even if that delicate prospect doesn't bother you, you're still stuck making a lot of phone calls.

You have no further responsibilities to anyone—not for plane tickets, not for anything. Your guests' inconvenience at your postponement is nothing compared to the inconvenience you will suffer if you enter into marriage at the wrong time. You must be happy. That is key.

POST-POSTPONEMENT INVITATIONS

Dear Elise,

My daughter and her fiancé postponed their wedding only a few weeks before the date. I called all the guests to notify them. Now that there is a new wedding date, we are wondering what sort of invitation we should send out.

—Shifting Plans

Dear Shifting,

I hope you've recovered from your marathon phone session, and you should be congratulated on your correct decision to make the calls (though it was perhaps above and beyond the call of duty to make them all yourself; this is a job that can be shared).

Everyone knows that the wedding has been put off; so when you order new invitations, don't worry about the language. Since everyone is in the know, you can stick with the usual language, and you don't even have to mention the previous date. You are in essence starting afresh, with a completely new invitation.

Epilogue

The Honeymoon's Over: A New Beginning

In the introduction to this book, I said that weddings are endings as well as beginnings. There's no reason to get depressed about this (even though a little bit of postwedding letdown is common). You are embarking on something new—and that is worth celebrating, even if the wedding didn't turn out exactly as planned or events took a serious and unexpected tumble into a handbasket and went south.

Now you know when it is reasonable to say "no" to a bride, no matter how close your friendship, and how to gain perspective with difficult parents, cloying relatives, and needy friends. You have the ability to gauge what battles are worth fighting and when it may be best to acquiesce, and what sort of middle ground can be negotiated.

In most ways, the end of the nuptial season means that life can go back to business as usual. No bridesmaid needs to think about asking "permission" before getting a tattoo on her neck; everyone can stop dieting and embrace the pleasures of chocolate once again; the bride and groom can go back to being as indecisive as they were before they finally made up their minds to get married. But etiquette should not be swept to the curb like so much tossed rice.

It should become a new companion, a set of tools much more universal than anything anyone was forced to admire at a honey-do shower. Of course it was useful in the intense wedding atmosphere, when everyone was examining your every move, but consider how handy it will be at dinners with your wife's possessive family, baby showers thrown for near strangers, the unfortunate day your supervisor decides to celebrate your pregnancy by calling you "Fatso," or that moment in the office when you realize that your promotion isn't happening and everyone is watching to see how poorly you'll behave. Etiquette will be your sword and especially your shield in the sandbox and in the boardroom.

But I'm getting ahead of myself. The wedding is still the magnet in your mind, bending all other thoughts or plans in its direction. Whether this distraction is delicious or encourages migraine, now you can rescue yourself from the trauma of being an abused bridesmaid, exploited father-in-law, reluctant bride, doormat groom, or disgruntled guest. There are ways to negotiate almost all potential horrors so that you can either get what you want or position yourself so you won't be up for nights on end having fake arguments in your mind with people you thought you loved dearly. There is always recourse for every scrap of indecision and some gesture you can make that will keep you from feeling utterly ground down.

In the end, etiquette, common sense, and the willingness to choose your battles will save your sanity, so take these seven lifelines and memorize them, turn them into little needlepoint cushions, stick them under your pillow and dream about them, do anything to keep them in mind. If you can't get the most specific protocols of etiquette to work for you, these little beauties will come through. And never forget: Weddings should be pleasurable, so enjoy yourselves.

When All Else Fails:
The Tiny Commandments

Smile sweetly. It is much harder for people to be nasty when you're happy. If you're worried that your ideas will be met with ire, insist that you're extremely pleased. "I'm so happy we're getting married in blue jeans. It's exactly how I've always wanted to do it." The less defensive you are, the less naysayers will be able to say anything obnoxious without looking shrewish themselves.

Keep your eyes on the prize. Even if you're the bride or groom, you don't have to control everything. The key to sanity preservation is to pick a few nuptial elements that are most important to you and guard these decisions with your teeth and claws. They can be anything: your choice of music, wedding dress, location, religious affiliation, color scheme, reception cuisine . . . anything. Then, be prepared to "share" other duties and decisions with relatives who insist on participating. You don't have to give up your opinions, but you'll seem so much more reasonable and agreeable if you give over tasks you don't care so deeply about. The alternative is to have meddlers trying to stick their fingers into everything.

Express yourself. It's unlikely that you or anyone connected to the wedding is psychic. Everyone, from the wedding couple to the guests, should be very clear about communicating his or her needs. You may not get what you want, but you'll spare yourself the frustration of wishing people would just read your mind.

Don't take it personally. Do not assume anyone is trying to offend you. Sometimes potential guests can't make it. Occasionally good friends can't be invited. Some people won't travel without their children. Space limits sometimes get in the way of single guests bringing dates. If it is too much to compromise, guests can always send a nice present and stay home, and the wedding couple can be glad of having some people to call up after the honeymoon who won't have already heard or witnessed all of their nuptial stories firsthand.

Be consistent. If you invite one single person to bring the date of his choice to the wedding, all unattached guests need to get the same courtesy. You can't handpick (as much as you would like to) which children are invited. If you've taken an active interest in one of your kids' weddings, try to manifest the same interest in your other children's nuptials. If you have been a bridesmaid six times before, you still need to participate with some enthusiasm if you agree to be in a seventh wedding. Feelings are easily damaged when people can tell that you've treated other people with more attention, care, and interest.

Etiquette is not a weapon. Don't correct someone's manners (unless you're that person's parent or guardian). That, in and of itself, is utterly unpleasant. And don't use etiquette as an excuse for acting like a spoiled brat. If you're a bride who doesn't get the tea-party shower you wanted, but instead got cocktails at a bar with no party games, don't claim you're mortified because your fête violated the rules of etiquette. It didn't. If you're a guest faced with a huge demand for presents on an invitation, quell your scolding impulse and give (or don't give) anything you want. You'll only pick a fight if you start to criticize, and then you'll have to show up at a wedding to face some miffed and defensive friends or relatives. Etiquette helps to make people comfortable. It shows people how to behave in any situation and teaches them how to reach when others come up short. It isn't your job to teach anyone about manners. It you have them, you'll finesse the situation to disguise the absence in others.

Don't burn bridges. The only thing a wedding should be the end of is the single life of the people getting married. One should never act horribly because of a wedding—not because it's her "special day"; not because weddings remind him of his own romantic failings; not because the nuptials make her realize she is losing a son, more than she is gaining a daughter. When real life resumes, no one should be speed-dialing his psychiatrist for emergency therapy sessions and Zoloft refills. It isn't the end of the world; it's a wedding.

About the Author

nong other things,
or Indiebride. She
husband, two sons,